D0796962

Alexander Horstmann
Class, Culture and Space
The Construction and Shaping of Communal Space in South Thailand

Southeast Asian Regional/Cultural Studies Series

Alexander Horstmann is Visiting Associate Professor for Southeast Asian Studies at the Research Institute for the Languages and Cultures of Asia and Africa (ILCAA). His interests include borderlands, religion and inter-cultural relations in Southeast Asia. Among his books are *Japanese Anthropologists and Tai Culture* and *Integration durch Verschiedenheit*.

Alexander Horstmann
CLASS, CULTURE AND SPACE
The Construction and Shaping of Communal Space in South Thailand

Research Institute for the Languages and Cultures of Asia and Africa (ILCAA).

Preface

by GEORG STAUTH

In recent years the emergence of the 'Newly Rich' in Southeast Asian societies has been subject of intensive academic debate and empirical research. The majority of these studies have been located within the conventional perspective of structural analysis and change, and thus subject to its limitations. The idea that the rise of the new bourgeoisie in local societies and the accompanying expansion of the sphere of public communication would lead to the decline of authoritarian and military regimes has long occupied the attention of Southeast Asianists. It is important to consider the new class as part of the global challenge to local structures. However, it would seem difficult to postulate–as perhaps in Taiwan and in Thailand–a general trend towards a decline in authoritarianism and the pharaonic state. Religious fundamentalism and liberalistic movements among students and intellectuals were by and large interpreted as the cultural and political representations of a trend towards democratic change among the Asian Tigers. However, these movements were rapidly absorbed by the new middle class culture.

This study conducted in the Songkla/Patani border region between Malaysia and Southern Thailand may be regarded as a response to the conceptual deadlocks of conventional structural analysis. In particular, Horstmann's idea that the new middle class itself in relation to ethnic or religious impulses for cultural reconstruction and network formation could attain the status of a social movement in local contexts, is highly interesting and opens up the terrain for new types of combining social with cultural analysis.

There is a certain contradiction between the idea of a middle class social movement and what emerges from this study to the extent that the movements in newly emerging spheres of public communication remain intrinsically tied to contested local space. The author offers a fruitful solution in that he points to the process of symbolic struggle for local authenticity which seems to operate as a functional equivalent to conventional social movements in that it strives for the social recognition of minorities while at the same time leading to a rearrangement in the distribution of strategic social power.

From a German perspective, rooted in the theory of communicative action, it would seem appropriate to study local interaction with reference to a type of institutional dualism between state and civil society. However, in this study the author develops a different conceptual tool for understanding the broader sphere of structural influences. His perspective throws light on intrinsic logic of local cultural dynamics and power. In rejecting the perception of what would figure in conventional analysis as a traditional local community, he transforms local space into a strategic field of social analysis. Communal space turns into a stage upon which the relationship between religions, politics and life world, and specifically the religious, moral as well as the consumer cultural aspects of the new middle class are seen at work as they unfold. In line with his idea of a new social movement, Horstmann defines local space as an essential part of the new public, that is, as the space of symbolic competition, rather then the location of public speech. Interestingly enough, the movement unfolds by means of symbolic struggle.

While the concept of a local public delimits the conventional separations between the private and the public sphere, Horstmann speaks of a new field of social interaction where life style accounts for the rearrangement of individual and social interests. With this concept of social movement as a basis, the study inevitably throws light on the political processes of the local cultural field. It is undeniable, however, that the popular trend towards life style performance in local space is at the same time embedded in the global process of consumer culture and mass society. Paradoxically, then, globalization seems to be the intrinsic motive for the reconstruction of non-western ideas in local cultural practice.

The study analyses the Buddhist movement in Songkla and the Islamist movement in Patani as middle-class-based social movements with quite similar traits of self-awareness and community formation and at the same time the tendency to transform questions of life style into basic ideas for political and social legitimacy. This study makes visible the theoretical intransigence of 'space' with respect to social and cultural dynamics: symbolic competition over space–which easily turns into militant conflict–is a very specific and concrete category and, today more than ever, of general conceptual importance. This is not specific to Southern Thailand. However, a social cultural theory of space, such as that developed by the author, is of particular relevance to Southern Thai conditions, while on the other hand, as appears to be the case in this study, any cultural theory of locality cannot be taken seriously without a concrete description of the local context as such.

The question raised here is one closely and deeply linked to the problem of European self-perception and social theory: At certain stage of the study the question arises whether we can really differentiate today in a context of globalization between areas of strategic distribution of power by means of socially communicated space on the one hand, and socially contested localities on the other hand. The coincidence of both remains to be analyzed. Horstmann, in attempting to trace the dynamics of the symbolic and ideological, religious and ethical, of life style and idealistic struggles at the grass root level of a local society, develops with the necessary accuracy the tools to analyse the various components, forms and dynamics of the constitution of a new type of public sphere. Here, symbolic performance and representation of 'authenticity' rather then ideas and production of public speech seem to be at work. In showing the social impacts of this type of cultural transformation, this study is a strong contribution to the cultural sociology of space. The case studies presented in this volume relate to two places in Southern Thailand Songkla and Patani. In Songkla, there is a considerable portion of the new Muslim middle class escapes the rule of Islamic law and rigid rules of Islamic attire and lifestyle encountered in Kuala Lumpur or Penang. Driven by a nostalgic turn to secular liberties they frequent Thai and Chinese owned casinos and hotels. In Patani, a Muslim minority dreams of a golden age, of a Patani which was central to the expansion of Islam in the Malay Archipelago, surrounded by a moon landscape of Japanese-owned shrimps farms. Horstmann however attributes less importance to these nostalgic drives, believing perhaps such nostalgia could be read as the reverse side of movement and life style as he describes them. This is a conceptually informed contribution to the social analysis of the emergent middle class culture in borderline urban communities in Southern Thailand. In understanding the broader dynamics of local cultural drives, Horstmann contributes a pioneering study to local change in a time of intense globalization and a refreshingly new approach to research on contemporary Southeast Asia.

Performing the Malay Silat in Satun, South Thailand.

Preface and Acknowledgement

Many people and institutions have helped to realize this study, which is based on my Ph.D thesis at the University of Bielefeld (Horstmann 2000). The thesis was originally written in the context of the graduate school 'Market, State, Ethnicity' at the University of Bielefeld, the findings of which have been published in the volume *Integration through Diversity* (Horstmann/Schlee 2001). Both Prof. Hans-Dieter Evers and Dr. Georg Stauth provided more than the usual advice and moral support. I like to thank Hans-Dieter Evers for guiding me through his vast experience in Southeast Asian Studies and Prof. Solvay Gerke for her initial inspiration on the sociology of a middle class in Southeast Asia, which co-exists with an impoverished peasantry. Among the many people who helped me in Bielefeld, I like to single out Georg Stauth as a teacher of the sociology of culture and religion. I like to thank Dr. Suchart Sriyaranya for his gentle companionship during writing in Bielefeld. My gratitude goes to the German Research Foundation (DFG) for a generous fellowship, to the Friedrich-Naumann Foundation for sponsoring my participation in the Fourth Inter-ASEAN Seminar on Social Development in 1999 and to the German Academic Exchange Service (DAAD) for a post-doctoral fellowship in 2001. Further, I acknowledge the Asian Studies in Asia Participation Scheme grant from the Australian National University, which enabled me to organize a panel on border identity for the First Inter-Dialogue Conference on Southern Thailand in 2002. The Research Institute for the Languages and Cultures of Asia and Africa, Tokyo (ILCAA) provided me with just the best possible working conditions. I gave the thesis to competent readers in Thailand, Malaysia, Japan and Australia for feedback. Prof. Annette Hamilton (University of New South Wales), Prof. Sharifah Zaleha (University Kebangsaan Malaysia), Prof. Chaiwat Satha-Anand (Thammasat University) and Prof. Omar Farouk Bajunid (Hiroshima City University) provided stimulating comments. Their encouraging words urged me to go ahead with the publication. Obviously, I tackled questions that have not been dealt with before in the literature on Southern Thailand (but see Stivens 1998 and Kahn 1991, 1992, 1995).

I like to thank Dr. Ryoko Nishii for her invitation to ILCAA, her kind assistance during my stay and I am extremely grateful to ILCAA and its director, Prof. Koji Miyazaki, for accepting my book in its Southeast Asian Regional/Cultural Studies research monograph series (No. A 818). I also like to thank Prof. Christian Daniels for his assistance in his position as head of the publication committee at ILCAA. Special thanks are due to Yui Kimijima for his kind assistance.

I like to thank Dr. Karin Werner and Transcript Publishers for their superb job. I thank Karin Werner for everything.

Giving Alms in Kelantan, Malaysia.

This study on the cultural competition of ethnic groups, their symbolism and negotiations of power in Southern Thailand is based on ethnographic fieldwork with a spectrum of people who have hitherto hardly been seen worthy of ethnographic attention. Academics, teachers and intellectuals are themselves very much involved in the refashioning and production of cultural identities on the golden Malay Peninsula. Sometimes, I thought that this spectrum of people was too involved in the social poetics and politics of cultural distinction. Thus, I make no excuse of centering on the narratives, educated people deploy in their everyday negotiations of power. This approach takes Bourdieu's concept of 'Distinction' (1979) as a starting point and looks carefully at the production of the many little essentialisms that result in the construction of the self and the other. In particular, I was puzzled by the essentialist categories of Thai Buddhists and Malay Muslims and by the stereotypes and descriptions of their cultures, which, ironically resemble the essentialism of the nation-state and which seem to ignore the diversity and cultural complexity of the peninula at the Isthmus of Kra. This region has changed from a center of maritime trade, inter-cultural exchange and religious mission to a borderland, in which the people have become firmly incorporated into the space of the nation-state.

The focus on the educated middle class is violating a taboo. Social anthropologists and sociologists are expected to choose their village and to reproduce some of the myths and representations of Southern Thailand. But, following Herzfeld (1997), this cultural intimacy, which people like bureaucrats, artisans and teachers try to hide from the foreigner, is often the most interesting and revealing practice to be explored. Staying with my wife and our baby in Songkla and Patani, I found that some of the key codes which was structuring my fieldwork were the debates on morality, on family and the home, on sexuality and on gender relations. People were constantly talking about family and home. Debates on morality and the moral state of society obviously had an impact on notions of being a worthy person, of dignity and self-esteem. I noted the high emotions that have been linked to the organization of everyday life. This deployment of binaries of good and bad creates friends and enemies, people to be trusted and people of whom to be suspicious. The loss of comfort, moral security and the endless disruption together with the increasing presence of mass culture and cultural images of the West produce a melancholy, a discourse on authenticity, and nostalgia for the grandeur of the past, which seems so characteristic of the atmosphere reigning in Songkla and Patani as cradles of Buddhist and Islamic civilization.

During my 14 months fieldwork in 1995/1996, I became attached to the cultural complexity and beauty of the region and to the strong will (*hoa kaeng*) of its people. In following the cultural re-discovery of the people, I hope that I have not adopted the same longing for authenticity and nostalgia as my informants. I have to excuse myself for disturbing the private sphere and peace. I think that people are not used to speaking about themselves and their communication is often a discovery of the self. On subsequent visits, I became interested in religious networks, peasants and fishing households across the Thailand/Malaysian border. However, I kept being impressed by the escalation of identity politics and the emotions that were involved. I thought that I had to show the technologies of the self and the processes in which identities are negotiated. I found assistance in Herzfeld (1997) who argued that symbolism (social drama) should not be dismissed as mere anecdote and from two friends, who helped me during the critical stages of the fieldwork, namely Khamnuan Nuansanong and Wae-Maji Paramal. Both are willy-nilly participants in the identity politics of Southern Thailand, embracing reformist ideas in Theravada and Islam, respectively. It is to them that I owe all.

I am very lucky to have Naomi and I have seen my two children being born and growing up during the writing process. Naomi and Sascha have been in the field and have contributed considerably to the final product.

It is a great loss for me that my mother could not witness the publication of this book. It is to her, Karin Anna, nee Rattay, that I dedicate this study.

Alexander Horstmann, Tokyo, August 15, 2002.

Contents

Border Stories 2

List of Tables, Figures and Map

Figures

Introduction

Visions, Claims and Utopias

Map 1: Southern Thailand, showing Songkla and Pattani in the Gulf of Thailand

The present study is concerned with the escalating competition in which cultural concepts vie for hegemony in the expanding local public sphere in Southern Thailand. The aim of the study was to assess recent forms of we-group formation, which seems to be centrally based on the cultural imagination and distinction of the educated middle classes. The transformation of society and culture in Southern Thailand has rarely been explored from this angle. Buddhist-Muslim relationships and identity politics in the 1990s can be interpreted as resulting from the integration of Southern Thailand in national and global processes of change. The incorporation of the region into national and global spaces is a social process that leads to new forms of differentiation and distinction, not only for economic and political systems, but also for ethnic and religious communities (cf. Preyer/Boes 2001).

We want to turn the notion of globalization on its head by examining how the participation of the educated middle class is producing new zones of change and also new borderlines and new frontiers in social conduct. As the world-system expands, it incorporates new territories and new people. Southern Thailand is a boundary zone and a locus of resistance to incorporation. In this study, we explore how ethnic and religious communities in Southern Thailand are using social and cultural resources in local, national and transnational networks in their struggle for cultural distinction, thereby negotiating new borderlines and conditions of membership in local society.

Globalization is not a new phenomenon in Southern Thailand. The port on the Malaysian peninsula has been an important locus of education, cultural encounter and trade. It has produced a region of enormous cultural complexity influenced by India, China, Turkey and the Middle East. The incorporation of Southern Thailand into Thailand shifted the region from a center of the world to a border zone in the periphery of the nation-state.

The present study examines modernity from the angle of the educated lower-middle classes. This social segment comes about from the expansion of educational institutions, colleges and universities and the increasing plurality of education in Southern Thailand. We do not believe that globalization is a process that miraculously draws people from locals into a homogenous world, but, rather, it is a process that results from the initiative and creativity of people. The educated middle class are at once a powerful and a less-powerful group. They are powerful, because their educational capital provides them with a privilidged position in the cultural field. They are less powerful because their modest income limits their influence in the economic field.

Morality and Politics in Southern Thailand

It is from this context of accelerated change and the globalization of ethnic/religious codes that we re-examine the rise of ethnic and religious emotion in Southern Thailand: it is as women and men are discovering themselves in the numerous discussions with the researcher. The educated middle class is at home in educational institutions, comprising universities, research institutes, religious institutions, foundations, colleges, government schools, and Islamic schools. In addition, women and men are activists in charities, associations, Qu'ran reading groups, social networks, meditation groups, non-government organizations (NGOs) and in the media. The emergent educated middle class coexists with an impoverished peasantry and occupies a space between big power and the mass of rural smallholders.

Lifestyle groups develop a moral crusade as a priviledged project of ethnic groups in Southern Thailand. The structural change of the public sphere is being indicated from the angle of the moral state of society.[1] Lifestyles are becoming issues of political legitimization. In developing discourses on moral boundaries, the players present powerful standards of esteem and contempt, in which they distinguish the friend from the enemy. The question raised here concerns the rationality of the accentuation of cultural orders. What is the significance of a guided walk to a forest *wat* and its reporting in the local radio station? What is the significance of the spectacle of a public prayer in Patani Malay language and Qur'an citiations, in which life conduct is embodied? In short, this study is sensitive to the symbolic worlds of the educated middle class and their spectacle of authenticity. It examines the practices and symbols that inter-cultural communication uses at this point in time.

State of the Art

Chavivun (1993) points out in a review article on social sciences in Southern Thailand that studies on inter-cultural relationships are needed (e.g. Nishii 2001). Social sciences in Southern Thailand have concentrated on the traditions, folklore and arts of the region. This has produced some essentialised characterizations of Southern Thai identities and ways of life. In many works, scholars on Southern Thailand have taken culture for granted and present cultures as authentic cultures. Political considerations haunt the quality of research on Southern Thailand and continue to do so.[2]

The Institute of Southern Thai Studies in Songkla, without doubt the leading research institute, has focused on the documentation of Southern Thai history and culture, and links its research activities with the museum.

In this regard, Chaiwat (1992) argues that studies on Patani in the 1980s are political stories in which heroes and villains can be identified and in which academic and intellectual circles are, as we shall see, active participants as well as innovative agents in the representation of reality.

The master-discourse in Southern Thailand concerns the nationalist question and the reproduction of national intimacy in everyday life. The government has never been very successful in incorporating the cultures of the south into the nation-state. The south is an ambiguous landscape in which Thai civilization ends and in which another history begins. Taking this ambiguity of national intimacy as a starting point, the focus on inter-cultural communication is crucial. In the identification and presentation of the self, the other is always present. While Buddhists and Muslim cross in everyday life, people very much live in separate lifeworlds and choose their friends from among their ethnic peers. The other is not to be trusted. Everyday interaction reinforces this narrative of 'us' and 'them'. It is as if the national border between Thailand and Malaysia is multiplied on many levels of Southern Thai society.

I saw the whole zone of Southern Thailand as a borderland and have organized my empirical data around the question of cultural boundaries between the cultural segments of the Thai Buddhists and Malay Muslims.[3] In reflecting the multicultural character of the south and the political arenas and social struggles associated with it, this study focuses on the communication, plurality and work in which cultures are negotiated and made up.[4]

Communal Space

'Communal Space' here refers to an associative, communal framework, in which activities can be carried out, in which practical knowledge can be recorded and in which a project can be pursued. An analysis of communal space requires an understanding of how participants utilize resources, cultural or symbolic, in the transmission and preservation of power and practical knowledge; how organizational arrangements of the association affect the continuity, encouragement or obstruction of the participation by leaders, followers, friends and members; how the members constitute or re-constitute their identity in public life or beyond: and how the community and its activities are linked and articulated with power relationships and the discourse of the state.

The study is particularly attentive to the social class of people who organize themselves into new forms of sociability, such as neighbourhoods, friendship circles, networks and communities and to the inner life of these spaces. The public sphere cannot be reduced to an idealized communicative space, in which a reasoning educated class openly exchanges views about power. Locally-based social movements display a variety of performative expressions in the public space, which has been overlooked in general discussions about civil society. This includes visions, claims and utopias, which are communicated in the public space through cultural and religious performances.

Wat Phra Kho, Reliquia, Songkla, South Thailand.

Visions, Claims and Utopias

Southern Thailand is one of the main zones of contact between the main cultural worlds of Southeast Asia, namely the Malay Islamic and Thai Buddhist worlds. Indeed, the regional conceptualization of 'Southern Thailand' itself is problematic. The borderlines of the south as a region are constructed and reproduced by the Thai state and by Thai national institutions and organizations (Thongchai 1994, Bowie 1997). Much of the literature fails to make the problematic representation of Southern Thailand a conceptual starting point for the analysis of its multi-ethnic society and political arenas. The landscapes of Song-kla and Patani are localities which are affiliated with strong emotions of belonging and home. The Thai-Malaysian border slides well-established kinship relationships and religious networks. Social and cultural relationships across the border continue to be meaningful and the moral communities criss-cross the political boundaries of the Thai state.

The present study, exploring as it does the cultural arenas of Southern Thailand, is concerned with the many new and unchartered cultural territories that question, subvert and counter the official discourse upholding hierarchical traditional cultural values, officializing and legitimizing political ideology and suppressing cultural differences. Especially in the past two decades, Thai culture has been undergoing a process of redefinition and reshaping and the hierarchical top-down ideology has been rapidly losing force. The case study aligns itself with the approach of scholars who show that the opposition between strong centralizing forces and weak local resistance is ideologically loaded and needs some rethinking as regards the complex mechanisms by which local players filter national imageries according to their specific needs. However, the nation-state is not the only game in town.

Cultural globalization has unleashed a strong cultural dynamic, which leads to the contestation of development models and to a negotiation of Westernization. This case-study aims to show the complex and ongoing negotiation and reconstruction of Thai-ness and national identity and the contested nature of provincial identities in one region.[5] While the post-colonial school has underlined the hegemonic and dominant location of national culture with regard to minority cultures, this case-study understands Thai-ness as an important site of social struggle.

Stivens (1998) provides an approach going beyond the public/private divide. She stresses that anxiety about gender relations is a central characteristic of many Asian leaders and of the principal cultural contests in the region (Stivens 1998: 2). Gender relations, women's sexuality and ideologies about family and domesticity emerge as important fields of cultural competitions. Stivens shows that contests around the private spaces of modernity are dominant issues for the educated who are reworking ideologies about gender and the organization of the family and that the so-called private sphere has become a key site for the expression of the ambivalence about modernity. The ambiguous private sphere emerges as a politicised field, which is no longer a private sphere, but a contested issue in the public arena, with frequent debate in the media about the pressures and costs of juggling work and home, the nature of family life and proper and good Asian families and lifestyles.

This argument about the negotiation of the so-called private sphere on different levels of society links the private family to wider society and appreciates the multilayered complexity of political reality; this includes political action in everyday life and the symbols and rituals associated with everyday political actions (Gledhill 1994). Feminists have pointed to the multiple and shifting connections between the private realm of the household on the one hand and the market and state on the other: Sen/Stivens (1998) argue that such dualities (private and public) are collapsing completely in the modern world. Instead, they suggest that: 'the construction of these supposedly private spheres has been a very public process in which state, economy and religion have all played extensive parts' (Sen/Stivens 1998: 4). The example of Southern Thailand, shows how much the private has become a key site of social competition and how much the so-called 'private' sphere has been politicized.

Journalists, artists and academics, among them many women, are simultaneously creating, living in and contesting their own middle-class cultural forms. As Purushotam points out, the compliance of the lower-middle classes with the 'normal family' is not just produced through repression but through other far more subtle means, "including rising affluence itself and women's own policing of their ongoing construction of a middle-class way of life" (Purushotam 1998: 10).

Furthermore, the private is a highly politicised and contested agenda in the new social movements in Southeast Asia. Being a pivotal nexus between the local and the global, private issues, such as the family and 'correct' life conduct, play a crucial role in the self-definitions of religious and cultural movements, which are popular among the educated middle classes. The speakers for the Buddhist and Islamic movements are the representatives of their cultures, which are increasingly defined by family, gender and sexuality.

This study highlights the construction of morality as a key field, in which the segments of the educated middle class are articulated and make themselves visible and in which the borders of the others are developed. It shows that the people themselves are actively involved in shaping the cultures of Southern Thailand.

Previous Studies on the Middle Classes in Southeast Asia

Table 1. Share and Growth of the Middle Classes in Thailand:[6]

	1960	1994
Thailand	15,2 %	30,4 %

Source: Pasuk/Baker (1997: 32).

Recognizing the negotiation of identity, Kahn turned towards a concern with the textual qualities of accounts of other cultures and of the knowledge in the society that produces it. Kahn has argued for a definition of the middle classes that relates them by reference not primarily to the relationships of production, but to the processes of modern state formation in the colonial and post-colonial periods. The site for the production of cultural images is to be in the political arena, in that nexus of relationships of power forged by modern state formation between employees of the state and civil society.

The questions are how are cultural images actually produced, how and by whom are the same cultural images contested and what alternative concepts of culture are being developed? What has to be explored are the social spaces of local movements in which the production and consumption of 'cultural images' can be realized. The cultural images of culture and modernity are being developed by Stivens (1998a) who asserts that gender relations are absolutely central to the making of the middle classes. She is especially interested in the terms under which women as a category enter into public discourse and rhetoric about national and ethnic identity within present-day reworkings of national and ethnic imageries. Stivens hypothesizes that the recent politicization of gender is tied to ideological remakings of the private/public divide within late modernity. The current reworkings of domestic ideology are key aspects of the cultural production of the new indigenous middle classes.

Stivens' inclusion of gender relations and current reworkings of the public/private divide among Malay Muslim middle-class women is taken up in my chapters on the negotiation of the family, the consumption of cultural images and the making of moralities among young middle-class families (see Chapter 2). Stivens discusses the negotiation of gender relations among Malay families and shows that discourses of sex, gender and modernity are to be understood at the nexus of relationships between family, religion, nation and cultural globalization. The public spheres are conceptualized as public spaces in which gender relations are a site of conflict, contestation and inherent outcomes. The perception of the family as a fundamental institution of values in crisis is in particular is a key subject of legitimizing discourses in neo-Buddhist as well as Islamist discourse. I show that the production and consumption of cultural images translates into frugal lifestyles according to role patterns of popular religious and political leaders and intellectuals (such as Chamlong Srimuang, Prawes Wasi and Nik Aziz Nik Mat).

Lifestyle is a significant mode of social integration that is increasingly moving to centre-stage: why does lifestyle move to the centre-stage? One of the main arguments put forward in this study is that private and public spheres are increasingly blurred in modernity, making the private a highly politicized issue in the extended public sphere. In ignoring the private, and in separating the cultural from the political, Rüland (1999) seems not to be able to to catch the centrality of the new culture for the identity of the middle classes. Can it not be that the middle classes forward their own visions, claims and utopias, thus providing the state with additional legitimacy or contesting the political ideology of the state and its cultural politics?

The formation of the cultural identity of the middle classes can also be considered in a context of globalization. One of my aims is to reject simplistic arguments on the global homogenization of middle-class lifestyles (Robison/Goodman 1996). Instead, this study underlines the importance of culture and religion as important social fields in which alternative modernities can be expressed. Cultural images about life as a central cultural code are not only entangled in global networks and ideas, but also enter global cultural communication and in large part contribute in structuring global we-group formations.

Basically, the performance and demonstration of cultural images is seen as a process of communication and lifestyles are a central cultural sign with which the culture of the middle classes can be communicated in the public sphere. The focus is rather on the politics of everyday life and on the ways in which the identity of the middle-classes is negotiated in a particular setting at a particular historical juncture.

In Southern Thailand, cultural images of the good life are matched by lifestyles as blueprints for the organization of everyday life. Local signifiers are not replaced by Western symbols. Islamic or Buddhist networks, for instance, are rapidly extending to a global scale. The middle classes participate in the dissemination of new patterns of lifestyle and life-conduct. Lifestyles are systems of reference that in the case of the cultural periphery can be powerful markers in which alternatives to the Western models can be expressively identified. Kahn notes that not only have the symbols of culture entered all areas of public life, but the cultural arena has itself become intensely politicized. Thailand and Malaysia are currently awash with symbols of traditional culture. Symbols of traditional culture are being used by the state and by the middle classes alike.

Religious Self-Affirmation in Southern Thailand

Any analysis of religion in Southern Thailand must first note the coexistence of the Buddhist and Islamic religious fields. Theravada Buddhism is the official religion of Thailand. Buddhism is also an ethnic identifier that is closely associated with notions of Thai history, customs and selfhood as is Islam for Malay identity. This study looks at the contemporary religious tensions between the revitalized and globalised forms of Buddhism and Islam. This study in particular highlights the privatization of religion in Southern Thailand in the communities of Thai Buddhists and Malay speaking Muslims.[7] In Asia, the processes of secularization and rationalization have stimulated the growth of charismatic forms of religion among the emerging middle classes (Lee/Ackerman 1997). In Southern Thailand, Theravada Buddhism has been secularized, whereas Islam has not. For Buddhism, Songla and Nakhorn Sri Thammarat represent centres of Theravada, but also a border with Islam. Malay speaking Muslims in Patani are culturally bound to the Islamic strongholds of Kelantan and Trengganu on the east coast of northern Malaysia. The study is interested in exploring the practices of self-affirmation, the individualized appropriation of religion, the chanelling of globalized networks and signs into local Buddhist and Muslim society and the use of religious forms in the cultural competition.

Taking issue with the production and consumption of cultural images, I will show the positionalities and politics of representation in competing public spheres that themselves have become arenas of competition and contestation in the transformation and global re-construction of locality. The aim is to present a more comprehensive and fine-grained analysis of sociocultural changes in Southern Thailand.

Mosque, Langkawi, Malaysia.

Outline of Chapters

The book is divided into 3 Border Stories on Buddhist Muslim relationships in south Thailand, highlighting the crucial role of educated individuals in the resurgence of cultural and religious forms and in the escalation of cultural competition in south Thailand. The purpose of Chapter 1 has two related concerns. First, it provides a historical backdrop to social and cultural change. Second, the chapter drawas on the narratives of typical middle class men and their concept of a 'worthy person'. A 'worthy person' corresponds to certain moral standards, which are defined and contested by Buddhist and Muslim segments of the educated middle class. Chapter 2 looks at the birth of consumers in south Thailand and portrays some families and their personal negotiation of cultural images about good life. I argue that the self and identity are increasingly defined through practices of consumption.

Largely unnoticed by the literature, social and religious networks have been established in Songkla and Patani. Chapters 3, 4 and 5 are devoted to the presentation of the Thai Buddhist people's organisation in Songkla (*Klum Rao Rak Songkla*) and to the presentation of Islamic movements in Patani. From a dramaturgical perspective, the city becomes a front stage. Urban life is like a play in which roles are distributed and in which people engage in symbolic interaction. Strategies of selfhood–individual and communal–are explored in these movements where the so-called private sphere becomes a politicized subject of public concern. At first sight, the practices and discourses do not allow for comparison. But a closer look reveals striking parallels: both movements centre on models of legitimate behaviour and life-conduct, on the access to education and knowledge and both movements develop sophisticated patterns of social organisation and leadership. Activities are organised by a core group of leading local intellectuals who adopt the role of a parent. Both movements develop patterns of mobilisation and discipline of new members. Both movements recognise the increasing importance of the cultural market. Culture in this process becomes a key element in the negotiation and contestation of new class relations and the genesis and change of society more generally. By realising cultural productions, the socio-religious movements are increasingly able to set the standards of legitimate models of behaviour. The leadership is upgrading the cultural field, thereby creating and defending a communal space which is steadily nourished and supplied with the movement's own media/knowledge/cultural material. In the process of constructing and conceiving space, new positions emerge in the social arena which are being occupied by the new class of educators. The production of small-scale community media is absolutely central to the articulation of the socio-religious core groups and their members. Community media, private radio, print media, pamphlets, brochures and videos provide a new dimension to the making and distribution of public opinion. The role of the community media are analysed in Chapter 4. Social memory is central in the making of a society and in the production or challenging of the social order. Southern Thailand's cultural heritage becomes part of culture as a contested space. In the politics of selective remembering and forgetting, middle class agents become archaeologists, historians and architects of collective identities. The appropriations of partial interpretations of Southern Thailand's history constitute a crucial part of cultural identity assertion. The re-enactment of the past in commemorative ceremonies and bodily practices is shown in the second half of Chapter 4. The identity politics in Southern Thailand are taken up in Chapter 5. The concluding remarks provide a summary about how the cultural segments of the middle classes discursively construct, contest and re-imagine Southern Thailand in pluri-cultural society and political arenas.

Border Stories 1

1

Locals and Cosmopolitans in Southern Thailand

Chaiyan Rajchagool (1994) notes that the view that Bangkok occupies the solar position, holding an entire system of regional satellites together, reflects the fact that the working of an ideology has continues to dominate Thai studies. The Thai nation-state is relatively recent. Siam became a nation-state only in the early 1900s, when Bangkok suppressed the autonomy of the outlying regions in the north, the northeast (Isan) and the south. The articulation of state power at the local level required the creation of a state apparatus and the appointment of commoners to state personnel. In social terms, the growth in the numbers of state personnel meant the emergence of a new category in the social structure. This new category comprised what was referred to literally as royal servants (*kharajchakan*). In practice, these people were the building blocks of the new state. They formed a special social group, distinguished by their skills and state functions. The appointment of commoners to office and function produced considerable tension with the old *Sakdina* system, the essential feature of which was the rigorous partition of classes by birth. The new service rank order opened up the possibility for the *phrai*, the commoners, to move up the social ladder. In the face of Western colonialism, the state apparatus was organising the rural population in the outlying regions more tightly. The new administrative units were state authorities in the making. The structure and expansion of the bureaucracy, which was set out during this period continues in force to the present day.

Before the nation-state, an entirely different concept of statehood prevailed in Siam and in Malaysia. The traditional Southeast Asian state, or *negeri*, was a different kind of entity. Its borders were shifting and permeable. As Anderson (1983: 41) has written:

"The territorial extension of the state is always in flux; it varies according to the amount of power concentrated at the centre ...

the kingdoms were regarded not as having fixed and charted limits, but rather flexible, fluctuating perimeters."

The Thailand-Malaysian border has sliced well-established kinship and ethnic ties across the border on the Malaysian peninsula. The local perception of the border differs substantially from central views (Carsten 1998, Horstmann 2002b). With the nation-state firmly in place, networks across the border persist and some were revitalized in the 1990s. In this chapter, the transformation of the region from the edge of commerce and religious education to a modern borderland at the fringe of the Thai and Malaysian nation-states will be investigated. The current movements in the borderland are best understood in this historical frame.

At the Religious Crossroads

The changing plural ethnic system in Southern Thailand is on the religious crossroads between the Thai and Malay cultural worlds. The golden peninsula has drawn a multiplicity of ethnic groups to its shores during the course of the past two millennia (Ackerman/Lee 1988).[1] The population movements along the coasts and through the forests of the golden peninsula produced a religious tradition remarkable in its complex diversity. Seafaring Indonesians, Indians, Arabs, Chinese and European migrants, merchants and missionaries in search of trade and salvation left their traces on the plural ethnic system in this part of the world. The strands comprising the region's rich religious traditions included animism, Buddhism, Hinduism, Islam, Christianity, and various forms of Chinese folk religion. Buddhism and Hinduism provided ideologies and symbols that enhanced centralization of political authority during the early period of state formation on the peninsula. Islam was ascendant in the Malay world by the fifteenth century. European colonial domination beginning in the sixteenth century gradually created the basis for a larger scale political entity, tightly integrated into world-markets.

Buddhism in Thailand

As one of my key informants put it, the Buddhist monasteries formed a bloc against the penetration of upper Southern Thailand by Islam. My informant told me the story of a highly charismatic abbot, Luang Por Tuad, who could transform sea water into drinking water. In the south, the Buddhist monasteries play a central role in the reproduction of the nation-state and Thai ethnicity. Early in the twentieth century, with the restructuring of the administration and the establishment of a territorial state, all monasteries across the kingdom were integrated within a single administrative organization through the Sangha Act in 1902. From this point in time, salvation was only being possible only under state Buddhism. The unification of the many dispersed monasteries brought individual monks under the control of the legitimizing authority of the King. The overwhelming majority of the Thai population is Buddhist. These figures provide the statistical backing of the ideology that Buddhism is the religion inherent in the Thai nation (*satsana phut pen satsana pracham chat*). Buddhist villagers associate Buddhism with all rites of passage that colour their everyday life. The childbirth ritual, for example, includes a recitation of the *Namo* (*Namo tassa bhagavato arahato sammasambudhassa*). One month after birth, a head-shaving ritual (*kon phom fai*) is held and monks are invited to bless the child. The passage of time is also marked by the holy days (*wan phra*) and the Buddhist festivals. The *Sangha* assumes a special role. It is only through the *Sangha* that the Buddha and the *Dhamma* finds expression in society and it is through the *Sangha* that they are transmitted. New Buddhist movements in the 1980s and 1990s in Bangkok have questioned the monopoly of salvation (Taylor 1990). As pointed out by Fukushima (1999), Santi Asoke's ideology is radically different from the dominant interpretation. The development of ascetic practices and the staging of Buddhism as a social virtue in the public sphere are of great appeal to the educated Bangkokian. The development of a frugal lifestyle fills the spiritual need of the Bangkokian middle class by allowing the privatization of religious practice. Santi Asok and Thammakai provide a forum of social organization for Bangkokians who are looking for alternative strategies of constructing selfhood in a changing Thailand.

For the sophisticated urban middle class, reformist monks provide alternative role models for morals (*sila*), salvation and discipline. The reformist monks in modern Thailand have been introduced by Jackson (1989). While placing considerable emphasis on the individual practice of morality and *vipassana* or insight meditation, the reformists approach practice from the viewpoint of Buddhist doctrine and reject the traditional village forms and the royal form. Phra Bhudhadhasa Bhikku is being called the greatest Buddhist philosopher and in terms of moral authority may have esily surpassed the top of the official Sanhgha. Bhudhadhasa Bhikku was born in 1906 in the Southern Thai province of Surathani where his Chinese father and Thai mother owned a store in the town of Chaiya.

The south is regarded as a centre of Theravada Buddhism and Ligor and Songkla are regarded as centres of Buddhist civilization. Yet, the south has a special position in Thailand with Buddhist and Muslim villages neighbouring each other and mixed villages, in which Buddhist and Muslim villagers co-exist. However, the interest for the other is giving way to avoidance and hostility in many places of Patani. Co-existence as a way of life has been captured by Nishii's seminal study on a Thai-speaking village in Satun province (Nishii 1999, 2001). Her work focuses on the ritual interaction between Buddhists and Muslims. Taking the relationship between ancestors and descendants (*chuasaai*), Nishii shows how villagers manage difference and how religion coexists in daily life. From her fieldwork on ancestor cults, Nishii argues that the coexistence of religions is embodied in ancestry. The relationship between ancestors and descendants is reciprocal. The social memory provides the basis on which communication is possible. Dancing *Manora* is a way of returning boon that have been requested. *Manora* is a local knowledge, which has been recorded by Muslim as well as Buddhist villagers. Focusing on religious ancestor rituals, Nishii provides rich data on their inter-cultural communication. In *chuasaii*, Muslim and Buddhist villagers communicate codes and symbols in a metalanguage, bridging religious differences.

Islam and the Malay World

As Muslim merchants extended their control over the Indian Ocean trade routes, Hindu and Buddhist contacts with the Indonesian archipelago dwindled. In the fifteenth century, Islamic scholars and missionaries were attracted to Melaka in increasing numbers as the population of foreign Muslim merchant residents in Melaka grew. The Islamization of the Malay Peninsula reflected developments in the Muslim world beyond Southeast Asia. Persianized conceptions of kingship as well as Sufi mystical doctrines preached by Muslim missionaries were compatible with the prevailing Hindu-Buddhist religious and political culture. Muslim reformers of the eighteenth and nineteenth centuries proclaimed Shari'a law as the foundation of the state. It was at this time that the Malays intensified their direct contacts with Islamic centers in the Middle East (Roff 1967, 1970).

Through greatly increased participation in the pilgrimage to Mecca beginning in the mid-nineteenth century, the Malays became aware of reformist doctrines. After completing the *hajj*, Malay pilgrims remained in Mecca for an extended period of study under well-known Islamic scholars,[2] some of whom were leaders of Sufi mystical orders (*tarekat*). The Nakshabandiya *tarekat*, which was influential among Malay pilgrims, taught an orthodox form of mysticism that strongly emphasized obedience to Shari'a law. Travelling Muslim scholars of local and foreign origin disseminated the new trends in Islamic thought on both sides of the Straits of Melaka, linking the Malays of Sumatra (Minangkabau) and the peninsula to the sources of Islamic reformism in the Middle East. The modernists, who sought to strengthen and uplift the Muslim community through purifying Islam propagated their ideas through new educational institutions known as *madrasah*, which were modeled after those in Cairo, and through the publications of newspaper (Roff 1967). Patani, in the early nineteenth century, became a centre of Islamic education for those wishing to study under the tutelage of the teachers at the mosque in Mecca. Its reputation was made by scholars of the Patani *ulema* and their classical works on Kitab Jawi, such as those of Shaykh Daud al-Fatani and Shaykh Ahmad bin Muhammad Zayn al-Fatani (Madmarn 1999): "His (the latter) brief biography tells us that he was born in 1856 in Jaring, Patani, and died in 1906. He was a descendant of a Hadramawt preacher who came to preach Islam in Patani, went to study at Al-Azhar University and returned to Masjid al-Haram, Mecca, devoting his life to teaching". The Islamisation of Patani can be divided into three periods: the 'magical period' from the late thirteenth century to the late eighteenth century, the theological period from the late eighteenth century to the 1920s, and the 'modern period' from the 1920s onwards (Kraus 1984). Shaykh Dawud and Shaykh Ahmad are popular to the degree that their books were published in Malaysia, Indonesia, Singapore and Egypt and that some of their works have been copied and reprinted from the nineteenth century down to the present day (Matheson and Hooker 1988). Most of the Kitab Jawi of the leading *ulema* of Patani were first printed in Mecca or Cairo and gradually moved to Singapore, then to Penang. The interest in Jawi books has not yet shown any signs of decreasing in despite the growing interest in modern Islamic media and in spite of the considerable presence of the Thai mass media. The traditional system of teaching is still being offered despite of the processes of change. The date of Patani's conversion to Islam is one of the political stories of the border. As pointed out in Chapter 4 on the structural appropriation of the past, the contestation of the past is part of the cultural construction of locality by the state and religious-political movements. The archeological work of Thai Buddhist scientists on Hindu and Buddhist monasteries, pointing to early Hindu, and Buddhist influences on the golden Malay Peninsula are being carried out on land. This memorial space is appropriated by Malay Muslim scholars who suggest that Patani was at the forefront of Islamic conversion in the twelfth and thirteenth centuries (see chapter 4 on Community Media and the Politics of Nostalgia).

Modernity and Religious Resurgence

In the current cultural competition between Thai Buddhists and Malay Muslims in Songkla and Patani, politicians, bureaucrats and intellectuals who are using cultural forms as a covert form of social action are politicizing religious identities. While previous studies have examined the coexistence and religious boundaries on the village level, this study is concerned with religious revivalism in subjective strategies and hegemonic communities of the educated middle classes and with the political purposes of cultural performances. It is my thesis that many scholars in the local arena who may have like to deal with this perspective are themselves players in the resurgence of cultural and religious forms. It is vital not to give another representation of Southern Thailand, but to try to get into the engagement of citizen with the nation-state. As Herzfeld does, we need to ask:

"What advantages social actors find in using, reformulating, and recasting official idioms (e.g. religious forms) in the pursuit of often highly unofficial personal goals, and how these actions—often in direct contravention of state authority—actually constitute the state as well as a huge range of national and other identities" (Herzfeld 1997: 2).

We are distancing ourselves from an approach that takes ethnic or religious identities as granted. As Chaiwat (1992) points out very aptly, the literature on Southern Thailand is full of representations that base themselves on the assumption of essentialised ethnic categories. Instead, it is vital to grasp the production and consumption of ethnic and religious identities in the political ideology and organization of the state and in the visions of social and religious movements. Lee/Ackerman (1997) point out that in the Asian revitalization, the increasing power of non-religious professionals and institutions drives the systematic codification of cultural identities and religious world views in the urban middle class.

"For the literate and technically proficient middle class, participation in religion often includes self-conscious reflection. The cultural traditions entangled with religion, as well as the religious beliefs themselves, become objects of reflection. The embeddedness of religion in culture invites identity-making activity as an extension of religious practice, which today has come to rely on sophisticated technical means for its consolidation and propagation" (Lee/Ackerman 1997: 9).

Lee and Ackerman assert that secularization and rationalization enhance and reframe religous action in Asia: cultural identities assert an ongoing connection with valued cultural tradition while engaging with Western modernity. In fashioning new identities, the middle-class participant is a producer who may draw upon popular as well as elite cultural elements and may fit these elements into an ordered intellectualized schema. We will see that the resurgence of religious identities for the middle-class participants in Southern Thailand is also a voyage of cultural rediscovery and nostalgia, in which the Buddhist and Muslim non-religious professionals engage with Western notions of modernity. In the religious field, local change is no longer considered in isolation from events in other parts of the world. The international electronic and print media play an important part in the process of ideological dissimination, just as preachers have increased the effectiveness of missionary work through jet travel and the use of sophisticated audiovisual equipment. Lee and Ackerman speak about a religious economy in the sense of a shifting supply of and demand for salvationary ideologies within a global context of competitive pluralism (Lee/Ackerman 1997: 9). In Songkla, middle-class participants draw on the personalized style of Phra Buddhadasa as well as on the local tradition of Buddhist monasteries in Songkla and Patthalung in their cultural rediscovery. In Patani, the transnational community of Malay-Muslim intellectuals draws on the Islamic party in Malaysia (PAS), on *dakwa* and youth movements of resurgent Islam and on new Islamic movements, such as *Darul Arqam*. In addition, the booming *hajj* business and the growing importance of Islamic education in the Middle East (especially Saudi Arabia) are Islamic networks that transcend far beyond the political boundaries of Thailand. The middle-class participants are gatekeepers who channel the global into the local. They are cosmopolitans with a keen interest in the world. Lee and Ackerman note that rationalization may become a tool in the hands of the Asian middle class for the organization of religious identities among members located strategically. Just as bureaucrats of the nation-state use religion as a central legitimizing resource, members of the educated middle classes in Songkla and Patani organize or consume heightened cultural identities from the religious markets.

The Sacred Landscape: Historiography of South Thailand

In her local history of Wat Phra Kho, Patthalung, Gesick (1985, 1995) balances her local manuscripts against national and academic historiography. She argues that as national geobodies were being mapped into place, local histories were literally being mapped out of existence. The local manuscript, the text, describes how the southern Thai landscape has been perceived and inscribed by the local people. The mind of the people saw the past embedded in a landscape, a landscape of enduring places indelibly marked by ancestral power. In the imaginings of the people of the Patthalung region, 'the area has figured for uncounted centuries as a land copiously imprinted with traces of the life and deeds of Lady White Blood, the mythic ancestress with whom all histories of the region begin' (Gesick 1995: 2-3).[3] Not only have the manuscripts been removed from the local context and shifted to the national center, but the historical sensibilities have also changed. Their preservation was informed by local stories about ancestors and heroes, 'whose actions imbued the local landscape with supernatural power and who could be communicated with through ritual' (Gesick 1995: 79). Gesick (1995) notes that the 1980s and 1990s saw a surge of interest in local history in Southern Thailand. Indeed, adopting Gesick's approach to historical sensibilities, the meaning of local history may also change in the local arena after high education and mass media as well. The past is now part of the cultural rediscovery of the educated lower middle class in Songkla and bustling Hadyai. The sacred landsape of heroes and ancestors has become a terrain for structural nostalgia and authenticity. Local culture provides the backbone of a reconstructed cultural identity in the Thai nation-state. A gilded replica of the *Sathing Phra* map dominates the museum on the handsome new campus of the Institute for Southern Thai Studies.

Family and State: Chinese Immigrants in Southern Siam

The development of Chinese capital in Southern Siam as a comprador to the Siamese state has facilitated the formation of a Chinese bourgeoisie in Southern Siam and the domination of the southern Siamese economy by family dynasties of Chinese descent (Phuwadol 1993). Jennifer Cushman (1991) has shown that the formation of a Sino Thai dynasty in Southern Siam went hand in hand with the interests of the central state in terms of tax revenue and social control. The success of the Khaw family, for example, was built from a set of interlocking and interdependent relationships that included kinship, economic and political ties. For the sake of its egoistic capitalist interests, the Khaw fam-

ily has been a faithful client of the Bangkok state. Reciprocity of
interest was fundamental to the revenue farm system on which the
Khaw family's fortune was based. The family's reliability in delivering
the money was rewarded with posts and appointments in the Thai bureaucracy. From the position of governor, Khaw Soo Chaeng was able
to maintain order in an unstable and distant region and to further his
family's financial position. The objectives of the Khaw family and
those of the state coincided closely. This relationship between the central state and Chinese business families is nurtured in the present and
is remembered culturally through the promotion of Chinese foundations and Chinese festivals and through visits of members of the royal
family to the memorials and shrines of Chinese families. Cushman
(1991) illustrates the choices that have been open to Chinese settlers to
secure their place in Thai polity. Service to the state led to the family's
rapid upward social mobility, freeing it from its immigrant roots and
tying it to the policies and strategies of the Thai rulers. Cushman (1991)
casts the family's history in such a way as to illuminate how the Khaws
used their political positions to advance the family's commercial interests and how King Chulalongkorn promoted members of a provincial
family with powerful economic connections to political positions in order to help consolidate the state's authority in an outlying region. Cushman's (1991) second theme relates to the strength of the family, which
it derives from its power bases in the Thai political community and the
Chinese commercial world in Penang.

First, Cushman (1991) illustrates how closely the state's political interests and Chinese commercial interests coincided and shows that
while the Chinese families certainly took advantage of the patronage of
leading political figures in Siam, they also had access to Chinese kinship
networks in Penang. As Reynolds notes, 'the account of the lineage as
a business is nested in the early formation of the Thai nation-state: The
Khaw lineage had a geopolitical position in Southern Siam and Malaya,
which the Siamese court in Bangkok relied on, even referred to, and
fostered' (Reynolds 1991). Cushman (1991) points out the family's
flexible response to any opportunity that could help family members,
Western, Thai or Chinese. In particular, she illustrates how the Chinese
community could be politically loyal Thais and still follows aspects of
Chinese ritual. They could choose Chinese or Sino-Thai spouses serve
as administrators in the Thai apparatus, as long as those alignments
served their subjective interests. Only the Western capital and colonial
administrations challenged the position of the Chinese bourgeoisie.
The Chinese entrepreneurs were in close contact with Western colonial
administrations and trading houses, adopting Western lifestyles, dress
codes and other forms of conspicuous consumption, such as playing

golf and tennis. Cushman's (1991) study also explains crucial patterns of class and strategic group formation in Southern Siam, especially illuminating the nesting of class formation and social mobility in the processes of nation-state building and globalization.

Stories from the Border

Patani is a disputed frontier. Centuries-old struggles between the Thai state and Malay sultanates resulted in the incorporation of the rebellious frontier into the Thai nation-state. Muslim separatism against the encroachment of the Thai state has strengthened relationships with the Islamic heartland in the Middle East and resulted in an unprecedented level of Islamic assistance to an area that was regarded as so marginal. The Malays in Patani regard Kelantan and northern Malaysia as part of their social world. The local perception of the border differs from the symbolism of the center. Islamic networks in Southeast Asia and to the Middle East change the meaning of citizenship. Malay-speaking Muslims have well-established kinship relationships and Islamic networks across the border. Many people from the Patani elite have chosen to live in Malaysia and to become Malaysian citizen. Kelantan has been the centre of political exile for the separatist movement in Patani. Many families are split between Thailand and Malaysian territorries and many of them have dual citizenship for convenience (Horstmann 2002a). Many Patani families send their children to Islamic schools in Kelantan because they worry about the Thai-Buddhist influence on their children. Lately, Patani has rekindled nostalgia for middle class people in Malaysia who join the Patani Malays in their Friday prayers and form circles on Islamic morality to authenticate their cultural experience. Arab and Indian merchants had settled in the commercial centres of Patani by the end of the twelfth century, intermarrying with indigenious people and forming the nucleus of a Muslim community. The Muslim kingdom of Patani grew in population and in prosperity. Patani was described as an important commercial port on the peninsula for Arab and Chinese traders. Ever since the establishment of Muslim dynasties, the kingdom of Patani seems to have experienced alternate periods of independence and Siamese control. At times, when Patani was under Siamese suzerainty, the sultans were obliged to send *Bunga Mas* (flowers of gold) to the Siamese court as a tribute and a sign of loyalty. In confrontation with British colonial expansion on the peninsula, King Chulalongkorn used the colonial technology of mapping, drew the Thai-Malaysian border in 1909, and re-organized the administration. The sultanate of Patani ceased to exist.

Malay-speaking Muslims are being marginalized twice over. They are being discriminated against in Southern Thailand and certain rights and state resources are withdrawn from them. In Malaysia, they are second-class citizens and are regarded suspiciously because of their socialization and accommodation in Thai society. The subsistence of Malay smallholders is threatened by the depletion of natural resources and the introduction of large-scale fisheries. The social mobility of Malay children in the Kampung is hampered by the socialization in the Malay world, the cultural distance to Thai teachers and enduring discrimination against Malay-speaking children.

In the 1990s, Patani witnessed a resurgence of Islam and a more firm integration of the region into national political and economic systems. The emergent Malay middle class is increasingly bilingual, benefits from the educational opportunities in Thailand and is attracted to a more orthodox interpretation of Islam and Islamic texts. In the representation of the self, Islam and Malay ethnicity is increasingly decoupled and Thai is increasingly influential as a medium of religious education. The Malay language is a tool of cultural distinction and is widely used at home, in the Islamic boarding schools and at the markets. Thai is pentrating the social world of the Malays in the form of television, newspaper, education, and popular culture. It is common for young Malays to spend periods of their education in Malaysia and to switch creatively between Thai and Malay worlds.

Entering the Scenery

Long before the Chao Mae Lim Ko Niew celebrations officially start, the sleepy Patani town busily prepares for the event, which attracts hundreds of spectators from Thailand, Malaysia and Taiwan. In the 'Visit Thailand' promotion, the Leng Chu Kiang shrine is publicised as a prime tourist destination. The godliness of Lim Ko Niew becomes a site of pilgrimage for Southeast Asian Chinese. Thai and Sino-Thai pupils present folk dances from Southern China. A special troupe from Chachoengsao Province performs the dragon-dance and occupies the streets, squares and bridges of Patani. According to data from the Tourist Authority of Thailand, Malaysians constitute the largest group of foreign visitors to Thailand: Singaporeans constitute the third-largest group of foreign visitors to Thailand. Overseas tourism is spreading towards the Malaysian border and is crossing the path of Malaysian tourism, whose centre is the bustling town of Hatyai, moving in the opposite direction.

As Chinese from Bangkok, Malaysia, Singapore and Taiwan feel attracted to the Chinese New Year celebrations in Thailand, the Leng Chu Kiang shrine becomes a theatre for identity negotiations of the Chinese Diaspora. Moreover, the godliness of Lim Ko Niew transforms it into a place of pilgrimage for the Malaysian and Singaporean Chinese at a time when the Chinese have to severely compromise their identity in Malaysia. The extreme popularity of the Chinese identity festivals in Thailand can be seen as going hand-in-hand with the Islamic resurgence in Malaysia, the new economic policy and the shrinking public spaces of the Malaysian Chinese. Indeed, tourism is partly developing into groups of friends made up of Chinese tourists from Malaysia. At the Chao Mae Lim Ko Niew celebrations in 1996, the present author met a Chinese group from Kelantan that attends the celebrations regularly. This gives them the opportunity to meet their Chinese friends from Malaysia and Singapore in Southern Thailand with whom they share the Chinese event, stay in the grounds of the temple building, and go shopping for Chinese foods. During the celebration, they will see their Thai Chinese friends from other towns in Southern Thailand, in Hatyai, Yala, Betong and Sungai Golok. The regularity of the travel results in a multi-national Chinese community with Southern Thailand as its base. This demonstrates how the emergence of extended milieus partly questions our understanding of tourism. In Southern Thailand, Thai, Malaysian and Singaporean Chinese can meet each other as Chinese. Thus, journeying and travelling becomes an identical practice.

The activities of Chinese philanthropic and cultural associations, of religious temples, shrines and religious festivals, the maintenance of Chinese cemeteries, the continuous presence of Chinese private schools, the social networks of Chinese chambers of commerce, clubs (such as Rotary or Lions), alumni associations and the communication in six Chinese dialects (apart from Mandarin) show that Chinese identity is alive in Southern Thailand. The Sino-Thai generation partly rediscovers its Chineseness in the Thai language.

Moreover, the Chao Mae Lim Ko Niew celebrations not only help the government to cash in on travellers' money, but also to confirm the historical patron-client relationship between the Thai state, the royal family and the Chinese community. As Chaiyan Rajchagool has shown in more detail, the Chinese community in the lower South was a crucial partner of the monarchy and Sakdina of Siam as soldiers involved in social and military control and as tax farmers in the economic exploitation of the tributary provinces (Chaiyan 1994).[4]

The aggressive promotion of tourism has contributed to the commodification of a curse among the local Chinese upon the nearby unfinished Kru Se mosque. Chaiwat reports that the legend, which was once an oral tradition, has turned into a written assault on the mosque as the house of God. The changing condition was perceived as a threat in the Malay-Muslim population. Kru Se mosque became a theatre for the renegotiations of Muslim identity (Chaiwat 1993). The activities of hundreds of Muslims who have offered their prayers at the Kru Se mosque in protest against the Chinese appropriation of sacred space have been closely observed by the National Security Council. In 1990, some organizers of the Dawah-Ansar Muhadjirun (remembering the Prophet's helpers in Medina and those who laid the way by following the Prophet from Mecca) were arrested. The events had a tremendous impact in the Thai newspapers, in comments and readers' letters. Chaiwat (1983) argues that the ancient myth has been reactivated at a time when the tide of the Islamic resurgence is being felt in the lower South. The demonstration of Muslim identity at Kru Se mosque is aimed at linking Pattani to the glorious past of the Malay sultanate of Patani and Langkasuka. The call for the lost state revokes the painful story of the Siamisation of the Malay Patani kingdom (see Chapter 3; Syukri 1985). For many Thai citizens, kingship has come to represent all that is sacred in Thai culture. The identification of the present king for the people is frequently staged in ritual, ceremonial and artistic shows. Sound-and-light presentations and elaborate fireworks are performed in every city and all civil servants, including university professors, are required to participate. The Muslim professors complain that they are forced to participate in government-initiated performances. This again confirms the prejudices of their Thai counterparts that they do not love the nation. Royal projects such as the informal handicraft education centre in Pattani or income-generating projects in Saiburi under the patronage of the Queen are supervised by provincial governments. The Queen has acquired a special significance in Southern Thailand and provides a figure to whom powerful women feel attached by strong emotional bonds. The grandmother of the Chinese Khunanurak family displays photographs to me, which symbolize the visit of the Queen to her and the shrine in her old Chinese home.[5]

One important dimension of the development of the master plan of the lower south is tourism. The treasures of Southern Thailand are now presented to the potential tourist on a map, featuring the cultural diversity of the South. The aim of the Tourist Authority of Thailand is to promote tourism, to develop the regional economy and to incorporate local tradition into the Thai national imaginary landscape. The Korlae boat race on the Nara river or the dove singing competition in Yala are illustrations of the folklorization of ethnic identity and the transformation of local symbols into tourist commodities.

The manifestation of Muslim identity reflects the symbiosis of the Thai government and the Chinese bourgeoisie, the concentration of the economy in the hands of Sino-Thai entrepreneurs and the marginalization of the Malay Muslim people. Second, it shows that the construction and revitalization of identity narratives are themselves a political action. Globalization facilitates the flow of religious and ethnic identity in many ways and puts the the borderland and the revitalization of identity in a new spotlight. Far from being new, religious identities are the product of century-old struggles.

Playing for a Muslim Wedding, South Thailand

Sketching the Landscape: Some Illustrative Vignettes[6]

This section opens with biographies that illustrate the location of the middle class. The ethnography compares how (male) members define what it means to be a 'worthy person' (Lamont 1992).

These short vignettes aim to illustrate some typical features. The middle-class and upper-middle class men occupy new positions in society. The important transformation concerns the rise of a new strategic group of professionals, medical professionals, architects and engineers, entrepreneurs and civil servants. One feature of all men in our sample is the exercise of power. This power is exercised on different levels of society. Clearly, however, the men take leadership roles in public life. Their intervention in society is legitimated by their educational capital, which in Southern Thailand is highly prestigious. In addition, the vignettes aimed to shed some light on the social habitus. The men presented have a clear image of a 'worthy person'.

This definition implies on the one hand a demarcated role at work and in the public sphere, but also the construction of symbolic boundaries with other classes, of feelings of inferiority and superiority and definitions of the self and the other. The growing self-confidence of the men is their social mobility, their achievements in personal life and their commitment in the public sphere.

This intervention in the public debate as well as their social standing is based on the increasing prestige of knowledge in society. More precisely, it is based on new systems of knowledge and professionalism which are being introduced into local society. These new pools of knowledge form the basis for fluid positions and new identities. The men are participating in different ways in public life in Southern Thailand.

The middle class is situated firmly in the local context. Significantly, as the Chinese entrepreneurs were situated strategically towards Western trading companies, the men in our sample serve as a mediator between local systems of knowledge and global systems of knowledge. Thus, the men become cosmopolitans with a keen interest in engaging with the world. It feels good to become cosmopolitan. The men carry with them the cultural baggage which they acquired during experiences abroad. They return home as learned and respected men who are able to channel the global into the local.

Somkiat

I got to know Somkiat in one of the workshops which was organized by Songkla Forum in a hotel at Songkla beach. The workshop, the organization of the workshop and its preparation is Somkiat's passion: a very gentle, open and generous personality, Somkiat engages himself and hopes to contribute something meaningful to society.

In addition, Somkiat's life project reflects a fragile balance between the loyalty towards his father and his desire to contribute something meaningful to society. Somkiat's intensive longing for a better society seems to me a nearly desperate expression for his wish of Somkiat to realize himself, in his own words, "to do something meaningful in life." Somkiat is longing to participate in this change, to be an initiator of this change and to take part in meaningful activities.

Somkiat is the descendant of a Chinese lineage in Hatyai and Sadao, one of the nine children of a Chinese entrepreneur and his four wives. Somkiat is the 'black sheep' of the Chinese lineage, because he is not a profit-minded person. Asked about his role in the family, he says that he gives little help in the business of his brothers, but he aims to represent 'the name' of his family in public life. His father is a Chinese entrepreneur who owns a casino in Sadao and who diversified into real estate and rubber plantations. Somkiat is managing the *mubaan jat san* for his mother; however, the business was hit by the economic crisis. In the eyes of his brothers, Somkiat is seen as a failure. Somkiat is also interested in doing business, but he aims to do business with a human heart. Thus, he told me that housing is a form of habitat, a way of life. In this sense, he wants to create a harmonious community by selecting the inhabitants. The cluster of houses could thus function as a community and everybody would support each other, the facilities provided by the company. In order to discuss issues of real estate, and ways of doing business, Somkiat invites entrepreneurs or professionals for informal talks at his home. Thus, a friend of Somkiat's, who has just returned from the United States, reported on his experiences and showed slides of house clusters as they are realised in North America.

Education plays a crucial role in his social projects. Somkiat took a B.A. at Ramkamhaeng University in Bangkok, and he told me that he always wanted to be a teacher. He has taken an honorary post in the Department of Business Administration at the Hatyai Campus. In addition, he helps in a project to reintegrate adolescents who have been in prison into society. Thus, Somkiat is always on the alert, prepared to join activities which he deems useful for what he calls a 'good society'.

Somkiat's projects include a private school, which he would like to design himself. He would like to dedicate his life to the 'future generation'. Somkiat is not opposed to the public school system, but would like to introduce some modern pedagogical patterns which he knows from the West. The school is one of his unfulfilled dreams. In addition, Somkiat has opened a book-store in which he aimed to sell good books, and invite the authors to public meetings; however, he found that his book-shop would only accumulate debt. Currently, he supports a local newspaper, called Focus South using the influential format of Manager Daily (*Pujatgarn*), and aims to create a platform for southern Thai audiences. Somkiat is travels regularly to Bangkok in order to meet his Ramkamhaeng alumni to learn from public life in Bangkok and to bring in similar activities to the South.

Somkiat says that he wants to be a person who is known to struggle for the good of society. He believes that people like him have to provide the seeds for a human social environment; he gives a picture of

Hatyai as a business city, contrasting it with the world in which he would like to live. In his words, "Hatyai businessmen are egoistic and in a state of fierce competition." The rich and influential meet in closely-knit circles, and are members of exclusive Clubs such as Rotary or Lion's Clubs.

Somkiat believes that a worthy person engages in the improvement of the self and of the society. While he does not question capitalism as such, he is looking for new ideas from his Bangkokian friends and tries to implement them in his 'place of birth' (*baan koet*). In fact, he regrets that his brothers are as materialistic and power-orientated as his father was. The social environment continues to be highly capitalistic, as Somkiat sees it. However, Somkiat feels comfortable in a role participating in voluntary organizations, and will be there, if new opportunities will open up. In this role he condemns the egoistic members of society who think only in terms of money. He is still looking for friends and for the fulfilment of his dreams.

Ismail

Ismail was introduced to me by a Muslim lecturer as the president of an association for Muslim businessmen. Ismail is a friendly, good-hearted person full of humour. Ismail is an upwardly-mobile trader who is expanding his import/export business to become a large-scale trader of frozen food. I visited Ismail regularly at his home-place. After a Friday prayer, I joined Ismail for a meeting on Islam ethics and morals. The session was accompanied by Malay healers who came from Malacca. The participants in this meeting aim to introduce an orthodox, intellectual, modern Islam as a life-form. I joined Ismail at his informal meetings with Muslim entrepreneurs where they discussed their situation as Muslim businessmen in combination with Muslim ethics. One of the subjects of discussion is the establishment of an Islamic bank. For Ismail and his friends, an Islamic bank would be an important step towards an Islamic economy. Muslim businessmen have to deal with Thai-Chinese banks. On the subject of banking, Ismail says: "Once you enter the bank you know that Muslim businessmen are not treated fairly." He says that Muslim traders have come to an understanding with 'stingy' Chinese middlemen in business life. However, he is particularly bitter about the Thai government. He complains that the government does not support them. From his point of view, the officials are corrupt, let themselves be invited to lunches, and generally, are not sensitive to Islamic culture.

In his own words, Ismail "dedicates his life to God". Therefore, while his world is that of commerce and business, he is eager to live up to his self-description as a defender of Muslim ethics: Ismail has founded an association of Muslim businessmen. This association in no way challenges the more established provincial chamber of commerce in terms of capital. However, from Ismail's perspective, it is challenging the moral codes and imposes Islamic ethics on business life. He points out that the association, while recent, enjoys considerable support from Muslim businessmen.

Ismail takes me to a friend in a local mosque. The meuzzin calls people to the Friday prayer. Ismail tells me that he aims to become a more knowledgeable Muslim and points out that the Malays Muslims have to struggle with the Thai political system. He complains bitterly about the local government, which does not help the Malay entrepreneurs, considering them pariahs. Because 'it is impossible to be Malay', they choose to be Muslim, Islam being the option for a modern identity. Ismail is proud to point out the progress of his own life-project in which he provides the best education available to his four children and is building a new house for his own family. The association of Muslim businessmen is raising a *Zhakat* from the donations of Muslim businessmen. Coming back from a business fair in Kuala Lumpur, Ismail states that Bahasa Melayu is attaining the status of a world language and Malaysia is quickly becoming a spiritual and economic centre of Islam. While the Chinese call the Malays Muslims 'lazy', Ismail would like to call the Chinese 'cheating' ('as people who would sell their own grandmother').

Ismail has woven close ties with his Muslim business fellows, being well-known in Yala. He points out that a 'worthy person' should be able to distinguish between heaven and hell, be faithful to his wife and be a good Muslim who fulfils his duties. Ismail is drawing cultural boundaries against Thai state officials and Chinese entrepreneurs, encapsulating himself in a Muslim public sphere, yet continuing his practical interaction with Chinese traders and Thai officials at work. Ismail is aware of his status as an entrepreneur who seeks to further his life project in taking a leadership role in his association for Muslim entrepreneurs.

Punrit

Khun Punrit has invested considerable time and effort to research the archives, to talk to family members and to screen the family's documents in order to publish the results in a splendid book about the Khunanurak family's history. In addition, Punrit and his brothers established a foundation to take good care of the Lim Gor Niew shrine, the Chinese places of worship, and the graves. The foundation coordinates the preparations for the Chao Mae Lim Ko Niew festivals. Punrit thinks that he deserves to be a leader in the community as he develops efforts to organize Chinese cultural life. The documentation of his family's story is a specific memory, which is reenacted into the present and supports the social reputation of his family. The hobby developed into a passion and the Punrit and his brothers have invested 5 years of research to publish the results in a book, which allows a rare glimpse of the life of Chinese traders at the turn of the century.

While the family wealth from tin mining has vanished, the successors have put in efforts to maintain of the social standing of the family where Punrit is an entrepreneur dealing in marble and granite. His father paid for an educational sojourn in the United States where Punrit took a B.A. in Business Administration.

While the Khunanurak family has seen better days as influential Chinese tax farmers-turned-capitalists, Punrit's brothers have completed a university education and have established themselves as a doctor in a Hatyai hospital and as a lawyer in Pattani respectively.

Punrit and his Thai wife have three children together. Punrit has not only built up considerable cultural capital, he is also organizing Chinese entrepreneurs in the southern provinces. Punrit describes himself as a Thai patriot. He is worried about the resurgence of Islam in Pattani. From his point of view, Islam fundamentalism is a threat to national security and to the social order in Thai society.

Punrit's parents have invited us for a Sunday brunch in their old house. There, Punrit's mother shows me the old Chinese furniture from China, the porcelain and the art and decorations, which show the grandiosity of the Khunanurak lineage. Moreover, the photographs on the walls show the Khunanurak family hosting the Queen and other members of the Thai royal family during their visits to Pattani. At the week-end, Punrit takes me to their old British colonial cottage in the mountains of Yala, which goes back to the good old days when the Khunanurak family co-operated with Western companies in tin exploitation.

Kruathep

Khun Kruathep has invited me to take a look at his work on urban planning in Songkla. He has painted a vision of Songkla as a southern tourist pearl on the board of his municipality office in Songkla. His driver and his van are waiting outside for us for a tour. He and his girl-friend are keen to buy land in the surrounding villages in order to de-velop apartments for Hatyai's busy people.

Kruathep explains to me about an ambitious bridge project on Songkla Lake. His plans to transform Songkla into a tourist resort do not permit the presence of slums. Kruathep wants to construct a mar-ket, which would create income opportunities for the poor. He looks down on the poor and says that everybody has to work.

His language competencies make Kruathep a cosmopolitan, with a keen desire to be in the world. His solid college education in urban planning makes him an indispensable expert in the urban planning of Songkla. Kruathep comes from a humble Thai family. Kruathep said that he took his destiny in his own hands. After his studies in a Bang-kok college, he got a scholarship to further his studies in France. His education and experiences abroad brought him the worldview of a cos-mopolitan with a glittery dimension. He is keenly aware of his educa-tional advantage in his hometown of Songkla. While he stays with his mother and sisters, whom he supports, in a simple house, he has be-come a very influential planner of Songkla City. The mayor of Songkla who depends on various consultants has given Kruathep full freedom to carry out urban development from the government's purse, a fact that Kruathep has not been slow to use for the development of his own company.

Kruathep has a clear description of what a 'worthy person' means. 'Worthy' means achievement and continuous development of the self. Kruathep believes that a 'worthy person' must be outstanding in social skills and expertise. His expertise in urban planning is in high demand. Kruathep socializes only with his peers; associating only with cultured people. His studies abroad make him aware of his being Thai, favour-ing a Buddhism which is more secularly orientated. Because Kruathep has moved up the social ladder, he believes in achievement through his own power. He is interested in developing Songkla into the pearl of the south and maintains that slums and peasants 'hinder' the modernisa-tion of Songkla and have to be eradicated. He wants to transform the slums into a big market that provides income possibilities for the poor. Kruathep situates himself in the elite circles of Songkla which have ac-cess to positions of power. Asked about his special relationship with the mayor, Kruathep said that the mayor trusts him. He feels that he has a 'mission' to carry out the modernization of his hometown.

Preparing Alms, Kedah, Malaysia.

Cosmopolitans and Locals

Thus, Somkiat, Ismail, Punrit and Kruathep become cosmopolitans with a keen interest in being in the world. According to Hannerz (1992: 252-256),

> " ... the cosmopolitan is a creature of the organization of diversity in world culture, and consequently deserves some attention, as a type."[7]

There can be no cosmopolitans without locals, representatives of more circumscribed territorial cultures. Hannerz (ibid.) argues that real cosmopolitans is a willingness to engage with the other, 'an intellectual and aesthetic stance of openness toward divergent cultural experiences.' Apart from the appreciative orientation, cosmopolitanism tends also to be a matter of competence. First of all, individuals have the willingness to seize opportunities to engage with transnational cultures. During long stays, or many short stays, they can explore another culture and build up skills more or less expertly within a particular system of meanings.

Hannerz argues that real cosmopolitans are never quite at home again; the cosmopolitan makes home one of his sources of personal meaning. As Hannerz (ibid.: 254) says, 'Home is not necessarily a place where cosmopolitanism is in exile'. However, Hannerz (ibid.) admits, however that there are various ways the cosmopolitan may relate to his/her locale: 'Or home is really home, but in a special way: a constant reminder of a precosmopolitan past, a privileged site of nostalgia'. Somkiat, Ismail, Punrit and Kruathep all returned home after a long sojourn in another culture. Home is a comfortable place with familiar faces, where one's competence is undisputed but where for much the same reason there is some risk of boredom. As Hannerz explains, there is an apparently paradoxical interplay between mastery and surrender here. But even this surrender is a part of mastery:

> "The cosmopolitan's surrender to the alien culture implies personal autonomy vis-à-vis the culture where he originated. He has his obvious competence with regard to it, but he can choose to disengage from it. He possesses it, it does not possess him. Cosmopolitanism becomes proteanism" (ibid.: 253).

The cosmopolitan picks up from other cultures only those pieces, which suit himself. In fact, cosmopolitans can be dilettantes as well as connoisseurs. In other words, there is some ambiguity here. Whereas in the host society some individuals may experience hardships in adjusting to another system of meaning, another language and having to cope with loneliness, they do not come back with empty hands. With their newly acquired skills and expertise, the sojourners experience intensive social recognition and prestige in their home society.

What is cosmopolitan can be channelled into what is local. Because he has been in another, separate culture, the cosmopolitan acquires a specialised stock of knowledge. This enables the cosmopolitan to become a broker, an entrepreneur who makes a profit. 'It becomes their speciality to let others know what they have come across in distant places' (ibid.: 54). The ambiguity between surrender and mastery, dilettantes and connoisseurs can be illustrated with the examples of some individuals. Khun Somkiat was an active student in Bangkok Metropolis, where he took a bachelor's degree in law at Ramkamhaeng University. Although he felt estranged by the anonymity of the megalopolis and dislikes the stressful pace of life, he nevertheless returns to Bangkok regularly to benefit from the opportunities offered by a World City. In Hatyai, Somkiat is a sought-after and respected intermediary, who is away giving a helping hand. He has also taken up an honorary post as a visiting lecturer at the Faculty of Management at Prince of Songkla University, Hatyai Campus.

Ismail has travelled to Northern Malaysia, Kuala Lumpur and Sumatra. He reports that his Malay counterparts regarded him as a second-class 'Malay'. Although Ismail had no problems communicating in the Malay dialect, he noted the differences between customs and language in Southern Thailand and Northern Malaysia. Nevertheless, Ismail will continue to visit Northern Malaysia in the future. Ismail is well informed about the IMT-GT project and the construction of an Islamic bank in Southern Thailand. In his home society in Yala, Ismail is well-respected for his social relationships with Malay-Muslim entrepreneurs and Islamic *ulema* in Malaysia.

Punrit experienced a culture shock in America and was also surprised to find Southern China in a state of despair and backwardness, despite his being well-versed in English and the bearer of Chinese cultural capital. Nevertheless, Punrit finds both qualities helpful in Southern Thailand, where he enjoys a high social prestige. At present, he is planning further excursions to Penang and Singapore to explore his family archives. In Patani, Punrit is a leader and node of communication with high social standing.

Kruathep had a long liaison with Western Europe. While he enjoyed a solid education in architecture, he experienced discrimination on the part of the private sector in France and Germany towards foreigners. Nevertheless, Kruathep mastered the French and German languages, learned to manoeuvre in another system of meanings and headed joint ventures. However, after his divorce from his Spanish wife, Kruathep returned to Songkla, where he is a much sought-after professional, well-equipped with foreign expertise, languages and social competencies.

In contemporary societies, mobility has become a primary activity of existence (Thrift 1996). Journeying and travelling have become an ordinary part of the everyday cultures of the new middle class. As can be seen from typologies of Somkiat, Ismail, Punrit and Kruathep, long journeys to other places have been crucial turning points and rites of passage in the life-courses and biographies of the parties concerned. Therefore, it is argued here that journeying and travel for education or work always include identical practices characteristic of the emerging travelling culture.

The reasons for moving for long durations or for many short durations are manifold: first, educational advancement is a prime reason to spend considerable periods of time outside Southern Thailand. Although the sojourn to another culture may involve some frustration, the rewards in the form of titles, diplomas and certificates more than recompense the investment made, because academic diplomas and language competencies are highly valued commodities in the home socie-

ty. Second, work is an important stimulus for journeying and travel.
Social networks are woven on the way and import/export or trade involve travelling. Third, people will travel to somewhere to see it. Travel
in this sense is continuous with status, and this kind of travel includes
a marker of status. Such practices include pilgrimages, religious circles,
study tours of museums and monuments or simply travelling for entertainment and pleasure. It is a crucial element of modern life to feel that
travel and holiday are necessary.

The cosmopolitans are more involved in transnational cultures
than others. This social class of liaison officers, or mediators, bridges
the gap between the transnational and the local, as Hannerz explains:
'Insofar as they have greater access to metropolitan culture than most
of their compatriots, they are the latter's informants about the world.
As cultural brokers they are in part gatekeepers, deciding on what gets
in and what will be kept out, ignored, explicitly rejected' (Hannerz
1992: 258).

The life histories and life paths of Somkiat, Ismail, Punrit and
Kruathep also mirror social change in Southern Thailand and the spatial strategies of Thai, Malay and Chinese middle class segments. It is
no accident that Somkiat moved to Bangkok, Ismail to Northern Malaysia, Punrit to Southern China and Northern America and Kruathep
to Western Europe. The micro life-stories of Somkiat, Ismail, Punrit,
and Kruathep reflect in miniature social change in Southern Thailand
as a whole.

First, journeying and travelling become part of the global projects
that locals harbour. Second, we may speak about an ontology of mobility. Third, and most important, the composition of social or mental
maps on the part of the cosmopolitans can be observed. The cosmopolitans travel on global maps across a world of social networks. These
personal maps, which enlarge with time and cultural contacts and connections bring the cosmopolitans-to-be to their distinctive places.
From here, national and transnational connections are emerging, demarcating separate routes, which link Southern Thailand to the world.
While the connections, social ties and networks may vary from case to
case, social patterns emerge that can be summarized in a map showing
the comparable practices that bring Malays to Mecca, Thais to Bangkok and Chinese to Penang and Singapore.

As a form of cultural brokerage, cosmopolitanism has a tremendous impact on the locality of the home society, which makes the locality an object of negotiation and reconstruction. The public culture is
intertwined with the knowledge that social players have acquired in
both local and global contexts. Migration and media are the forces that
cause conditions 'in which ties of marriage, work, business and leisure

weave together various circulating populations with various kinds of locals to create localities that belong in one sense to particular nation-states, but are, from another point of view, what we might call translo-calities' (Appadurai 1995: 44).

Extending Networks

The idea of home has to be divorced analytically from the idea of lo-cality. As Dürrschmidt (2001) explains, the notion of home no longer contradicts the notion of mobility, "for it derives from people's ability to make themselves feel at home at different places."

Furthermore, the unlinking of 'the locale' and 'milieu' does not nec-essarily imply 'rootlessness' or 'homelessness'. Rather, 'social relations across distance show the very ability of the individual to actively 'iden-tify home' in an ongoing construction and organisation of interlaced categories of space and time.' The 'personal milieu', defined as situated configuration of meaning and action, "is potentially stretchable across infinite time-space distances."

It will be argued here that the cosmopolitans are in a position to transform pre-existing cultural idioms and to create new identities and new boundaries. The rediscovery of Chineseness and the revivalism of Islam in Southern Thailand are given here as examples of the rise of cultural identities as alternatives to the landscapes of state-related na-tional identities. Chaiwat states that conflicts may result between the Malay Muslims, Thai authorities and the Chinese community in an on-going process of identity formation.

The personal networks across distance in identity formation illus-trate the economic, political and symbolic strategies of between the na-tion-state and cultural globalization. These cosmopolitans are establishing a public culture in Southern Thailand, in which private life-styles are a subject of public discourse and that this public culture is about the social spatialization and the shaping of cultural spaces, as noted by Chaiwat (1993). Moreover, in the process of appropriating identification, the players are constantly drawing boundaries to the cul-tural 'other'.

Children at Prayers in Narathiwat, South Thailand.

2

The Making of Consumers in Southern Thailand

This chapter will consider the people of Southern Thailand in terms of becoming consumers rather than being consumers. As in Goffman-esque society, social relationships constitute a stage upon which the social player presents a performance. Social success hinges on the presentation of an acceptable image. Image-management and image-creation become decisive in the organization of everyday life (cf. Goffman 1959, 1974). Conceptualizing segments of the middle class segments as communities of practice, our central preoccupation is with the inter-subjective appropriation of the label middle class.[1]

The Stuff of Middle Classness

The appropriation of the label 'middle class' involves everyday lifework to ensure the continued upward mobility. These three portraits of young parents in Southern Thailand show the fragility of making the right choices. For instance, the juggling of home and work in the life worlds of our informants shows considerable stress and anxieties about the entry into modernity and its costs (Stivens 1998a). The parents live with a fear of falling. That is, the everyday life of the families does not only include hope for betterment and consumption of better goods than before, but also include anxieties, sorrow and even a dread of the future. Why is this so? It is a fundamental fact of everyday life that the families have to deal with social insecurity. They know well that there is nobody who could help them after falling, or halt the momentum of downward mobility. In the following, I would like to draw on my empirical data to analyse the everyday lives of our informants, covering home and work, domesticity, family, and, most significantly middle class space.

Nongyaw and Sompong: The Family is one of Nature's Masterpieces

'The Family is One of Nature's Masterpieces' is written in one of Nongyaw's many photo albums. The photo albums feature the exceptional rather than daily life: the development of the children, family vacations and the graduation of the couple. The photographs, looming large on the grey walls, keep a record of rituals, ceremonies, and the family. The photo-album illustrates the care, time and effort that the couple and parents are willing to invest in the development of their children. The well-being of the family is very much in the centre of the couple's concern, being intrinsically linked to the local state. This prosperity is realized through a livelihood that is based on the expansion of the local state. Nongyaw and her husband, Sompong rent a townhouse in one of Yala's mushrooming townhouse settlements. For Nongyaw and Sompong the house is the centre of the private sphere and of family life. The house signifies protection, recreation and privacy. Thus, they are thus saving hard to become home-owners. Coming from a humble rural background, both Nongyaw and Sompong like to see themselves as a new generation. On their initiative, we paid several visits to Nongyaw's father in the Yala countryside and to Nongyaw's roots in the rural hinterland.

In her father's house at the district level, photographs again abound, although the choice of the photographs is more limited. There are large photographs in black and white showing in particular every graduation ceremony of no less than six children. There is a Chinese altar (Nongyaw's mother was Chinese): there is also a painting of the Thai King and of a famous Buddhist monk from a local temple. Nongyaw has grown up in a Thai, Buddhist village.

Nongyaw and her husband, Sompong put emphasis on their university education, which allowed them to leave the village for the city. As her father not without pride pointed out, he spent the little money he had to pay for the education of his children. Nongyaw entered the primary school of the local temple, followed by the government secondary school at the Tambon. Later, she passed the entry examinations and gained a bachelor's degree in liberal arts at the Prince of Songkla University. Nongyaw and her husband place great value on social security, which secure employment offers. In addition, they enjoy concessions on their rent and kindergarten fees. Because her husband is frequently absent due to his work schedule, Nongyaw has the added burden of doing her job and raising the two children, as well as cleaning the house.

Nongyaw explains that she and her husband are prepared to work to improve their livelihood. She says that two incomes are necessary to sustain their level of consumption (although she likes to have a break). Therefore, they have to invest in a child-minder who is looking after their small child. The family spends a large proportion of their income on education (and some families even go in temporary debt). The investments reflect the priority that the family places on education.

Among a number of tutorials, Nongyaw's daughter attends a special class in classical Thai dance. While Nongyaw does not speak much English herself, she wants to prepare her children for the future. Nongyaw is also booking piano lessons, which are now becoming available in the booming private schools.

Nongyaw enjoys watching soap operas, which she likes to discuss with her friends. Nongyaw is interested in children's songs and books to help her out with her children's education beyond the materials provided by the school. She is creating boundaries to the social other, saying that peasants do not pay enough attention to health and children's development.

Nongyaw and Sompong have to cut expenses in order to realize a couple of middle-class dreams. Their proudest possession is a Japanese car. As Nongyaw puts it, having a car is crucial, because otherwise they would have to depend on uncomfortable public transport. Unable, to pay a large sum, Nongyaw and Sompong pay for the car by instalments. They rarely go out to a restaurant (instead, they get their food from food stalls). Nongyaw buys a new dress every 3 months to wear to the office.

According to Nongyaw, she and her husband have a harmonious relationship. However, she complains that she is lonely with the children as Sompong's work involves long sojourns away from home. Nongyaw explains that the family has to be cared for, nurtured and protected from the 'bad' environment and bad influences from other children.

Nongyaw believes in the modernization of the country, loves the King of Thailand, the royal family and actively participates in the image-making government campaign concerned with the beauty and quality of life in Yala. In Nongyaw's version of correctness, loyalty to the nation-state and the Thai royal family is part of the duties of a good citizen. Nongyaw is a close aid to the mayor of Yala. She is organizing a public relations campaign for a model municipality.

Nongyaw believes that it is her duty to prepare her children for competition in their potential future careers, to nurture their talents and to urge them to be Thai patriots with a will to preserve Thai culture. Nongyaw's daughter performed her Thai dance on the occasion of the jubilee of the Thai king, also playing the monarch's classical and jazz compositions.

Nongyaw and her husband participate in the important events of the Buddhist calendar and maintain a friendly relationship with the local *wat* at her parent's home. Nongyaw regrets that the leading role of the Buddhist *wat* is declining. Nongyaw and Sompong are used to visiting *wat* Chang-hai and to washing their children in the sacred water of the saint Luang Por Tuad.

Nongyaw is optimistic about the efforts of the Thai government to achieve the standards of a modern country. She is ready to put her faith in the hands of the national leaders and believes that the mayor of Yala is a powerful and generous patron. She thinks that she and her husband are part of the efforts of the state to build a model city and to improve the quality of life of the urban population.

In a sense, Nongyaw escaped from the demanding manual work and poverty of the countryside. The family's livelihood depends on the welfare of the local state and felt the financial crisis intensively.

Nongyaw has an ambivalent relationship with her past. On the one hand, she wants to leave her past life in the village behind: on the other, she has nostalgic memories about harmonious village life. She believes that young people lack sufficient orientation and therefore turn to drugs. After some time, Nongyaw told me that she perceives the distribution of drugs as a real threat that makes her determination to look after her children well even stronger. Nongyaw sadly claimed that Thailand is now a poor country. Her wages arrive late and the cost of everyday life is higher.

Nongyaw has a strong notion of social order, which she wishes to defend. Thus, she argues that in a time of crisis, the warmth of the family acquires a special importance. She believes that she can trust her husband and opines that trust is crucial for any relationship. She states that the 'going out' of her colleagues is a bad habit and very dangerous to their families.

The family is one of nature's masterpieces. As long as Nongyaw and her husband can maintain their life aspirations, they can fulfil their definition of happiness. Nongyaw seems to be the more dominant and more outspoken person in the relationship with a clear plan about her future. Her loneliness is overcome by her focus on her children.

Varunee and Boonchu: The Family as a Castle

Varunee and Boonchu have bought a house on instalments. The double glass and the thick walls protect their house from the noise outside and the polluted air of the roadside. Nevertheless, the location of their house on a main road is convenient for their clients. The house functions as general office of an American insurance company as well a home. Inside, the air-conditioning ensures a constant cool temperature in the first and second storeys. As Varunee observes, the cool temperature is pleasing to her clients.

Varunee and her husband are living in Hatyai and work as professionals in the booming insurance business. Varunee met her husband during a student club excursion. She settled in Southern Thailand after her marriage to Boonchu, who comes from an old Chinese family in Patani.

Varunee sadly pointed out that Boonchu's mother did not like to agree to the marriage, because of her Thai origins. In her husband's family, Chinese used to marry Chinese: only in the current generation is this marriage pattern beginning to change.

Boonchu and Varunee both have Bachelors degrees, Varunee' being in accounting and Boonchu's in management. Varunee recounts that she was chosen by Boonchu during their student days. Varunee and Boonchu work and live together. Boonchu is the head of sales representatives in Hatyai. Varunee is his helping hand, his secretary and his accountant. As a working couple, their working life and the private sphere are blurred, because their income and bonuses depend on the number of new clients whom they can convince to buy insurance.

Varunee has no income of her own, but controls the accounting. She also controls what she calls home affairs; that is, she is simultaneously a mother, a housewife and a close aide to her husband. After long hours of working, she has also has to clean the house, because, she says, her husband likes the house to be tidy for himself and especially for his clients. She always accompanies her husband when they pay their clients a visit, because, conversing with other families, Varunee and her husband represent a warm family themselves and speak to the other couples, as woman to woman and man to man.

During the economic boom, Varunee and Boonchu were able to acquire a large number of new clients. As the advantages of the insurance are spread by word of mouth publicity, so potential clients appear. With the economic downturn, the number of clients is decreasing rapidly, threatening the insurance business. The couple does not know whether they will continue to sell insurance in Southern Thailand, because they must fear that the company will have to close some offices.

Varunee and Boonchu pass on a new philosophy about life to potential clients. Varunee suggests that only a minority with a proper level of education understands the importance of insurance. Varunee and her husband regard themselves as experts who inform other people about the various conditions of and opportunities for insurance. As pointed out by both Varunee and Boonchu, the idea of the life insurance reflects new patterns of the organization of life and life planning.

Varunee explains that the couple could ill-afford to take a break from a tight working schedule. Varunee gives her son to one of Boonchu's aunts to take care of, although, as she puts it, she has a bad conscience doing so. Varunee does not like the idea of a maid, because both Varunee and Boonchu dislike the idea of somebody sharing the private sphere of the home. Varunee believes that she would then have to look after the maid, which she finds unsettling. The couple prefer to stay in the context of kinship to organize baby-sitting.

Because their son is an only child, Varunee and Boonchu pay a lot of attention to him. Because the 'ideal' family has two children, Varunee feels there is a deficit, which is pointed out to her by Boonchu's mother. However, the couple argues that they are able to offer a good education and a bright future for their only child. Their only child is of great importance to them. She reads a good deal of literature related to her son's development. She told me that during pregnancy she had a nightmare that her baby may be abnormal and she is therefore very happy to see him in the best of health. Thus, the hopes and aspirations of the family are coupled with anxieties about the future.

Boonchu used to go to the English speaking Club in Hatyai and converse in English with foreigners. Varunee has studied Chinese and is giving classes in Chinese at a private school. Because Boonchu was brought up with Chinese customs, the Chinese language is important to Boonchu.

Boonchu actively participates in the Chinese festivals, the Chinese New Year, and the Lim Gor Niew celebrations. He showed me a photograph of himself participating in the Nine Emperor Gods' festivals in Hatyai, himself participating in the festivals. He is also a member of many Chinese cultural associations. Boonchu added that his informal contacts in the Chinese associations as well as the Chamber of Commerce help him in his business career. Varunee and Boonchu are keen patriots and identify with the destiny of the Thai nation. Once, we had been invited to a lecture on the economic development of Southern Thailand in the City Hall. When they heard that Thailand had impressive export and economic growth patterns, Varunee and Boonchu were very pleased.

Boonchu told me that he, as a head of the company, travelled to Bangkok, Europe and America. Boonchu acquired a sense of professionalism and Western leadership style during his seminars.

Varunee is nervous about being seen with another man. Boonchu likes to joke that Thai women are the best in the world and Varunee does not know where he goes with his colleagues in the evenings. Boonchu also has a habit of drinking whiskey, a habit that Varunee overtly dislikes. Her critical comments are a little rebellion about his consumption of large quantities of alcohol. Until now, however, she has not challenged the gender roles in the family. However, she may do so in the future, because she is not prepared to tolerate Boonchu's drinking or womanizing.

Somjai and Narongrit: Managing a Family

Somjai and Narongrit have realized their dream of a home in Patani. While Narongrit is working in Hatyai with a telecommunications company, Somjai and Narongrit stay in their house in Patani, which means that Narongrit has to commute every day.

However, because his family comes from Pattani, Narongrit feels at ease there. Somjai was the manager of the new condominium 'gold village' (*mubaan muang tong*) and sold the townhouse and shophouse units to merchants, civil servants and teachers. She had just been appointed manager of the sports club when she became pregnant with her second child and had to give away the job to a friend.

At this point, she planned to join the telecommunications company and to move to Hatyai. Somjai and Narongrit rented a bungalow in a Hatyai suburb and rented their house in Patani to somebody else. Somjai was known as a very able and disciplined manager of the *mubarn* and a close aide to her Chinese boss.

However, because her pregnancy was making her feel sick, Somjai decided to postpone her plans and to stay at home. Then Somjai had a miscarriage. This was a very difficult time for Somjai and she would not appear again in public for some time. She was not prepared to go through this experience again, but Narongrit asked her to try, because he would love to have a second child and a camerade for their daughter. Thus, Somjai became pregnant again and she had a difficult pregnancy. She could talk about her experience to the neighbouring families in the *mubarn* and to her doctor in a private clinic, but she could not discuss her sorrows with her female friends, because she was afraid of losing face. Somjai says that it is rather difficult to discuss personal problems with friends, because everybody is in a sort of competition and compares themselves to one another. Somjai rather hates the idea that other people are talking behind her back.

Although Somjai does not hold back with her opinion, she will follow her husband and will accept his decision. She prefers Hatyai to Patani, because of Hatyai's better infrastructure and shopping possibilities. In particular, Somjai liked the atmosphere in the *mubarn* and the chatting with her neighbours. However, she willingly followed Narongrit when he wanted to return to their house in Patani, because, she explained, the tenant of their house did not take care of it, and they had better look after the house themselves.

In their leisure time, Somjai and Narongrit like to stay at home. Indeed, they hardly leave their house. Narongrit's brothers and sisters are frequent visitors. Narongrit was brought up in a very strict manner; his father was an officer in the Thai army who he had hardly knew. Possibly to compensate for a cold childhood, Somjai and Narongrit would like to build a warm family (*krobkrua thi obunjai*).

While Somjai is ready to accept the authority of her husband, she does not stand for her husband going out or drinking alcohol. In return, she is willing to take care of the household and to look after their daughter.

Somjai does not like to associate with the Muslim population. She believes that the Muslims cannot be trusted. She also thinks that the Muslims have bad habits. She points out that her neighbours are Thai like themselves and that they help each other out in need. She is afraid that something may happen to her daughter.

Somjai only permits her daughter to go in her parents' car or to play with her little friends in the garden of their house. She cannot stand the idea that women are selling their bodies. She also feels very concerned about male promiscuity, but thinks that this is happening in a world apart, not in her life world.

Sida and Sarunee: The Islamic Family

Sida and Sarunee are torn between traditional and modern lifeworlds. Sida and Sarunee live in Sida's father's house. Her father is a guru and a representative of the local mosque. Sida confirms that her father is a follower of the traditional Patani ulema. He converses in Melayu only. His house is located in a Muslim milieu. While Sida's father is a religious man, he eagerly supports the non-religious careers of his children.

We join some friends to visit the young couple and stay for a Malay-Muslim dinner on the floor of the living room. More friends are arriving. The house is open to kin, neighbours and friends. Sidah's father has just come out from the local mosque. Before he is served by his wife, he waits until we have finished eating. Sida is a nurse in the public hospital. She shows me the photographs of her recent wedding. The bride and groom wear traditional Malay clothes. Music and dance were not permitted. Explaining the marriage ceremony to me, Sida points out that only the husband is asked to confirm to that he will take care of his family.

While Sarunee received his training in Kuala Lumpur, he is employed as an engineer in Bangkok. Sida dislikes Bangkok, which is a foreign country to them. Kota Baru and Kuala Lumpur are like home. Sida stays in Pattani to help her parents and enjoys her work in the hospital, although she can see her husband only on the weekends.

Sida has worn the veil since childhood. She argues that the veil helps and protects her to be a good Muslim and to be firm in her belief. Sexuality is not to be judged negatively, as long as it is between husband and wife. Sida and her husband do not want to have more than two children. Sida would give up work and would support her husband if her husband would asked her to do so. Yet, the couple depends heavily depends on two incomes and Sida also would not like to lose her work and her friendships with her collegues, Buddhist and Muslim.

Sida invited us for *Hari Raya*. However, the celebrations in the kampung have been kept low key, however, contrasting with the colourful celebrations in Malaysia. I was told that the Muslims in Patani keep a low profile or joined their sisters in Malaysia. Sida has joined a group of young educated Muslims that aims to support Islamic education in the countryside. I have accompanied the young women and men of the group on their trips to the villages. The men speak to the villagers about the value of Islamic education. As Sida points out to us, the villagers lack teachers, materials, and money. Sida believes that she has a responsibility to help other Muslims who are less fortunate. In addition, the group has a wider aim to support Islamic education along the new standards of Islam as well as keeping the Malay language and the Jawi script alive.

Juggling Home and Work

Normative, patriarchal family ideology allows women to imagine themselves to be on a normal life-trajectory, in which they must work to acquire status as girl, young woman, married woman and mother. In doing this work, "the woman becomes of her own accord a key producer of middle class life and of her husband's and children's middle class life in particular" (Puru-shotam 1998: 136).[2]

In our sample, this work is naturally subscribed to women. Women have to cope with long working hours, and, after coming home late, have to clean the house. As one informant, a bank employee says: "My husband, a Chinese, likes to have the house shining. Just have a look at my hands." Nongyaw travels from the child-minder to the kindergarten and to work and, afterwards, to the supermarket. She also has second thoughts about giving her child to a child-minder, because she thinks that by doing so, she is not a good mother. It is remarkable that middle-class families do not look for maids to help them in the maintenance of their tight schedule. However, as the women point out, reliable maids are hard to find in Southern Thailand, because the demand for maids is recent. Moreover, maids would add to a long list of costs. The women further objected that they would not like the idea of having somebody else living in the same house. There is a middle-class discourse on the problems with maids. One has to take care of the maid; the maid disturbs the private sphere; the maid cannot replace the mother and so on. Varunee and Somjai rely on kinship relations and give their child to a poorer relative. Relatives can hardly refuse their moral obligations to look after the children of their richer relatives. The juggling of home and work, the burdens of women as working women and housewives and the unremitting struggle in a competitive economy are necessary in order to guarantee continuous ability to pay for the participation in a consumer lifestyle, consuming education, identity and modern life.

Moral Panics

The couples aim to fulfill the demands with which they are addressed as parents by the discourses of the governments, media and religious movements that centre on the family. The couples build walls around themselves in order to protect the family from harmful influences. Our informants had clear criteria to define good people and to distinguish them from bad people (*khon dii, khon mai dii*). The qualities that are attributed to good and bad are markedly gendered:

Somjai needs to know her husband's every move and would not tolerate him going out in the evenings without her being informed. Going out at night is associated with commercial sex.

Varunee complains about her husband's bad habit of drinking alcohol. A good husband does not waste the money meant for the mortgage. A good husband is the breadwinner.

Nongyaw is upset about the husband's long absences from home. A good husband stays at home. He is a family-man, as Nongyaw puts it.

For Narongrit, his wife should bear the difficulties of her pregnancy to give him a child.

For Sompong, Nongyaw is responsible for the welfare of the children.

For Sarunee, Sida looks after the household and prepares the meal in the evenings. In a life-world which is known for insecurity, prostitution, and pollution, the notion of being *khon dii* is upheld.

It is easily understood that women are more involved than men in the discourse of *khon dii* who contrast their life worlds with a world of loose relationships, minor wives and mistresses. Many female informants have expressed a strong fear of infidelity and HIV/AIDS, whereby going out is related to prostitution.[3]

There is a discourse of middle class women about prostitutes. Here, the *khon dii-mai dii* separation finds its strongest expression in distinguishing between good women and fallen women. Apart from the habits of going out and leaving the wife behind, women are especially nervous about extramarital affairs.

The horror scenario for women is a divorce. They can ill afford a separation from their husbands which would involve the loss of everything. Thus, the fallen women are perceived as a threat to the integrity of the family. Women feel concerned that their husbands cannot resist the offers of easygoing women. The fear is so real that women put up with the long absences of their husbands, cope with their multiple roles as mothers, housewives and working women, and, reluctantly, even tolerate drinking in order to guard their husbands within the bonds of the family.

Therefore, gender arrangements in middle-class life worlds are tight. Women adjust to the normal family ideology and do not question their role in it as long as the image of the family can be sustained and the hope of upward mobility is kept alive. The only reason that justifies separation of the couple is work. The women in our sample were careful to sustain the image of a good woman and accordingly, avoided being seen with men other than their husbands. As Stivens (1998a, 1998b) points out, sexualization of women in the discourses of the media and religious movements is prevalent and has no small part in the process of polarization of good and bad women.

The field of gender relations and a woman's place is increasingly politicized. In this regard, the heavy attack of the Islamic resurgence on the promiscuity of Thai men is getting additional momentum through the AIDS epidemic. Moreover, as we have seen before, the Thai family is read as being in crisis. It is this argument in which Malay-Muslims claim moral superiority. While the sexual division of labour is most pronounced in their families, and no claim on egalitarian rights is made, women do not have to win the affections of their husband. In contrast, there is a keen awareness in Thai and Sino-Thai families of the so-called crisis. Thus, the demonstration of the intact family in friendship groups is part of the everyday work of middle classness.

As a result of the steady making up of an image, the families find themselves in isolation. While women in particular are looking for female spaces in friendship groups, gossip in friendship groups and working relationships is often found oppressive. This is because it is not sufficient to have upward mobility. The fruits of the labours also have to be shown off and demonstrated in public spaces. Thus, the nightmare of one informant that her child may be abnormal is not least due to the fear that she could not present a healthy child to her friends.

The women find themselves in a vicious circle, in which they observe each other's development, in which they compare each other's progress, and in which they find it increasingly difficult to share their sorrows even with their best friends. Because work, home and child-rearing often occupy most of the family time, loneliness with pressing problems is not uncommon. The story of Somjai is a case in point. Instead of seeking assistance from close friends during her pregnancy, Somjai relied on other neighbours in the *mubarn* or on the aid of her doctor. As the breadwinners of a normal family, it is unthinkable for women not to work. This means that unemployment would have drastic consequences for the level of consumption and, indeed, on the self-perception of the normal family.

Practices of Consumption: Housing

Purushotam (1998) writes that social bodies are located in corresponding socially recognizable spaces. This was also my approach to social spatialization. The space that is recognizably middle class, " ... gives to the actors embedded in such spaces the self-awareness of their middle class position" (Purushotam 1998).

The concept of the habitat describes the spatial distribution in the urban landscapes and is most clearly expressed in housing. Construction, real estate and speculation are some of the visible dimensions of an anarchic capitalism and the expansion of markets.

With the emergence of a new estate with disposable incomes, the demand for suburban, middle class housing has risen and has encouraged potential landlords to join the real estate business. Housing both describes the spatial settlement and a dominant *genre de vie*–a form of life: housing is the visible marker of the arrival and expansion of a new social group as a result of modernization: the *mubarn jat san*, the *akarn-panit*, and townhouse, which find their origins in the classical Chinese shophouse, providing business facilities and accommodation and defining a life form in which Chinese settlers claimed spaces and created the urban markets.

One's social identity is to a great extent anchored in these territorial units. While villages remember a golden and harmonious village past, the new forms of housing are to be distinguished from the traditional neighbourhoods. While the people in the traditional neighbourhood share goods and services and leave the doors open, privacy and the privatization of possessions is the governing principle of the modern *murbaan*.

The habitat is not only a form of housing, but the very foundation of a life form. Bourgeois homes in Thailand have changed radically in the past few decades, and a totally new world has been created inside the walls of the home, which now has a dual function as stage and shelter. The *murbaan* imposes itself on the social environment as a purely spatial structure and as a social image. Housing is part of a lifestyle experiment that is made possible through globalization and mass consumption. The nurture, improvement and decoration of one's house is an identical everyday practice. The home-owner appropriates the living space and forms it according to his own needs. The inhabitants give their individual touch to the built environment, thus expressing their social status as well as their cultural affiliation. It is as if the families have to add their identical practices to an otherwise meaningless townhouse. Larger solidarities are expressed through the addition of an ethnic emblem. Chinese altars, pictures of King Chulalongkorn, pictures of Buddhist abbot Luang Por Tuad, and calendars with pictures of the royal family are added to the hi-fi stereo and TV sets and the identification, in which the old is linked to the new. The *murbaan* provides a social integration to the inside and a feeling of a 'we-group'. It is a dominant life form and spatial structure, imposing itself on the urban social system. The changing attitudes to the home also mirror the changing attitudes to family and nature and the changing perceptions of childhood.

The increasing importance of anonymity and privacy in the *murbaan* underlines the design of spaces by the new middle class and contributes to the making of an exclusive middle-class milieu. Thus, housing is thus a showcase for spaces of representation. The new homes represent a new living arrangement: the withdrawal into the new intimacy of the nuclear family. It is now possible to retire from the company of others. The increase in privacy is a result of the social reshuffle and the arrangement of social space. Thus, the new home thus separates public from private, servants from family and children from their parents. The campaign for bright nurseries reflects the changing perception of the meaning of childhood and of the meaning of parent-child relationships.

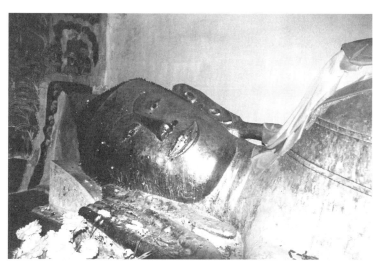

Reclining Buddha, Wat Sathing Phra, Songkla, South Thailand.

Changing Meaning of Childhood

Child-rearing, like gender arrangements and sexuality, is not just a matter for parents; instead, it is the concern of the collective. As Mulder (1997) has shown, 'Thai schools are producing the child the Thai nation desires'. What Mulder does is to explore the public world, that is, the ways in which schools propagate ideologies, nationalism, self-images and religious ideas. In a Foucauldian manner, then, Mulder is interested in the production of the docile body in the Thai school system. In the context under discussion, education is seen as a field of intense contestation. Here, I want to mention once again the arbitrariness of public private dichotomies and to explore the spaces of children's socialization in both the home and the schools, because we can assume that schools affect the household and vice versa.

The intensive care, the efforts, interest and time that parents invest in the rearing of their child is a strong identifier of middle-class mentality.

Chua (1999: 21) has pointed out that children's education is both symbolic and functional: "Children's education is both an investment in their future and a symbolic display of the parents' ability to pay" (Chua 1999: 21). Generally speaking, parents observe the development of their children closely and monitor their behaviour. A new child-rearing ideology has become general. The creation of specialists in relation to this indicates the rise of a new class and the creation of new needs: childminding for busy mothers, private tutorials in piano and English, and private lessons in Thai classical dance and classical music. Naturally, parents aim to provide the best education available for their children. There is a sense of competition from a very early age. In Southern Thailand, the educational landscapes are differentiated along public government schools, Chinese private schools and *pondok*.

The resources of kinship are limited as a result of new housing and living arrangements, so nursery schooling from an early age conveniently combines day care with education. In reality, preparation for university entrance examinations begins for parents with the nursery school.

The examination includes a long interview with parents and children. The interview deals with questions of child-rearing, living conditions, and occupational status. Thus, the parents, as well as their children, are assessed.

Once admitted, children learn their ABC and how to sing the national anthem or to play educational games. Everybody likes to have their children admitted to the demonstration and elite schools. However, because admittance is restricted, parents feel depressed when they learn that their child is not able to pass the entrance examination. The failure of their child adds to the anxieties of the parents and may raise the troubling question why are they beset by misfortune and what have they done wrong?

The fact that children are frequently in a state of exhaustion reveals the ambition that parents place on their children's education. The parents have understood that their mobility is due to their level of education. Accordingly, they may spend their tight resources on the children's education. Nongyaw hires a special teacher who gives tutorials in classical music and dance. Her daughter Pimai demonstrated to me her talents in Thai classical dance; she is going to take lessons in piano and English. Chinese children are taught Chinese customs and rules of behaviour. As for Malay children, they will learn Thai rather than Bahasa Melayu, go to a Christian school in the mornings and to a *pondok* teaching Islamic studies in the evening. Private tutorials in Thai or maths complete the day. Daughters in all families are accustomed to housework from an early age. Thus, gender roles are subscribed to girls and boys on from early childhood.

Projects of child-rearing must be seen in articulation with the reproductive process in which they are socially and materially embedded. The consumption of information on children's development in the forms of books and magazines, tapes with children's songs, and governmental brochures highlighting the baby's happiness, is informed and organized in close affinity with global transactions. The articulation combines local strategies of appropriation and global images.

Making up Domesticity: Emancipation and Subordination

First, practices in a number of fields show that dealing with insecurity about the right life model is a fundamental fact of everyday work on middle classness. People have only a vague image of the correct way of life. They have to deal with the specific political and economic conditions of Southern Thailand and thus are part of the overall social transformation. Their life planning is fed with considerable hope, aspiration, and ambition. However, as pointed out by our informants, the lifestyle experiments also include strong anxieties. Paradoxically, modern consumption in the fields of gender arrangements, sexuality, home, domesticity, child-rearing, and work is an experience of emancipation and, simultaneously, subordination (on this point, see Purushotam 1998).

Consumption: Life-Spaces of Self-Definition

Jonathan Friedman (1994: 16) envisages an approach that focuses on the ways in which reproduction is socially constituted from the vantage point of consumption: "By maintaining the general framework of reproduction we are able to situate consumption properly in a larger social field where it can be said to make sense in terms of the social strategies of a particular group.'

In modern forms of consumption, people appropriate the world in their own smaller space of existence and, importantly, take sides in a social struggle in an ongoing process of identity formation.

Nongyaw and Sompong: Thai Love Thailand

Nongyaw and Sompong enthusiastically embrace the propaganda of the Thai state aimed at promoting Thai culture. Tutorship in classical Thai dance and Thai traditional music illustrates nicely the efforts made for hierarchical distinction and the reproduction of Thainess in a minority situation. Their love for the Thai King also mirrors the dependence of their own life project on the modernization of the Thai state. The defence of Thai national identity involves distrust of Malay people who do not participate in the etiquette of the Thai state and are situated in a group of people "who are against us". Those people "do not respect the members of the royal family", are said to be "fanatically religious", they do not "speak the Thai language", 'they do not perform the Wai", "they do not pay respect to the Buddha image", "they do not obey Thai teachers". Nongyaw and Sompong believe that love for the Thai nation should be part of the school curriculum. Nongyaw and Sompong have a strong notion of good and bad people. *Khon di* help the Thai leadership to fulfil their development programme. Nongyaw and Sompong want to bring up their children to become competitive and patriotic citizens. Lifestyling reflects the appropriation of a world and is an expression of being *Khon dii*.

Varunee and Boonchu: Success and Ethics

Varunee and Boonchu in their practices of consumption aim to demonstrate success. Success is associated with hard work, discipline, order and tidiness. Varunee and Boonchu measure their success in terms of their house, their plot of land and their car. Hard work and professionalism are contrasted with the Malays, who are said to be 'lazy' and 'ignorant'. Varunee and Boonchu keep up a social order that they regard as taking care of Chinese values. Boonchu upholds the myth of the Chinese settlers who have built up the Thai economy and have created wealth. In this nostalgia for the good old times in which people used to live in harmony, modesty and simplicity are part of the Chinese-Thai worldview. This nostalgia for the community is compared with contemporary Southern Thai society which is read as being in crisis. Desire and corruption are seen as factors responsible for the crisis of Thai families, divorce and prostitution. Varunee and Boonchu aim to build a harmonious family, where modesty, wealth and harmony prevail.

A similar worldview is shared by Narongrit and Somjai. The family institution, its reproduction, the investments for the family's future and its protection is the base for understanding the practices of consumption and, sometimes, abstinence from consumption.

Sida and Sarunee: Following the Word of the Prophet

Sida and Sarunee borrow from the discourse of orthodox Islamic intellectualism. Practices of consumption are firmly embedded in a religious framework. In this framework, correctness in leading a life according to the guidance of the Prophet has priority. Islamic media, books, tapes and videos are consulted to distinguish good and bad and heavenly and hellish worlds. Veiling is a statement of obedience to the

rules that are set by the discourse of the Islamic resurgence. These authoritative codes are followed in food and dress. Islamic lifestyling involves strong practices of distinction and a demonstrative effect on the
Thai-Chinese. Taboos on pork and alcohol are followed, and are contrasted with the alcohol and drug addiction in the worlds of the 'unbe-
lievers'. The strongest boundary concerns gender and sexuality.
Sexuality is limited to the intimacy of the couple and compared with
the 'sexual promiscuity' of the Thais. Practices of consumption are embedded in a religious framework and contain a hefty attack on the lax
lifestyling of the Thais.

What are Collective Identities for?

As in other local contexts in the non-Western world, the cultural re-ori-
entation in Southern Thailand is intimately linked with the making of
consumers and lifestyles. I have aimed to shed light on the inner life of
the new consumers. Preoccupied with mobilizing the scant resources
they have, the middle classes in the making suffer from a fear of falling.
The new consumers are in a process of learning; their aim is to get access to what they regard as a modern life project. Their participation in
global life forms is perhaps more desired and imagined than real. That
does not mean that processes and shifts in consumption pattern are
not important. As Friedman (1994) argues, reproduction is socially
constituted from the vantage point of consumption. The socially deter-
mined habitus needs to be understood in that larger social context.

Consuming Thainess, Contesting Thainess

Practices of consumption 'make sense' in terms of the social strategies
of social groups. Strategies of self-definition as a cultural form ask for
cultural distinction and ethnic boundaries. From this angle, practices of
consumption can be read as statements that relate to the cultural images of the state, the media and religious movements. In particular, in
Southern Thailand, practices of consumption help to reproduce or
contest the hegemonic concept of Thai culture. Lifestyles such as
clothing and eating are linked with ethnic identity. New habitual forms
are important signs that are put into public spaces as ethnic emblems.
Lifestyles and practices of consumption are social strategies to define
the cultural self. The main argument is that strategies of consumption
are embedded into larger communal spaces and frames of reference
and representation that are shaped by the state and locally-based social
movements. Therefore, lifestyles are used to communicate loyalties

and identification. Lifestyles are communicators of cultural boundaries, in which cultural images of Thainess are either consumed or contested. As such, the lifestyles of cultural segments of the middle class
should not be confused with a growing homogenization of lifestyles, in
which local signifiers are replaced by Western symbols. Rather, competing constructions of the family show that lifestyles and new habitual
forms are important to processes of distinction and social integration.
They are important to processes of distinction, because they are powerful signs that are put into public spaces and negotiated there. Lifestyles greatly contribute to make distinction visible, and public. As we
shall see later, lifestyles are very important to the construction and
shaping of communal spaces. They are important to processes of social
integration, because they are part of a cultural whole. Thus, lifestyle is
integrated into metha-cultural systems of communication, in which the
families and cultural segments of the new middle class debate about
constructions of the family and good life. Doing so, they understand
each other well. Thus, all families bring their cultural baggage into the
public spaces. As consumers of cultural images, they all participate in
bringing in the private as micropolitics into the extended public
spheres. It is here that the organization of everyday life is linked with
the new quality of the extended public life, which is the main subject
of the following chapter.

Border Stories 2

3

Self-Affirmation, Globalization and Cultural Distinction in Songkla and Patani

Locally based social movements are central in producing cultural images of the extended public spheres. Looking specifically at the local reconstruction of culture, the Chapters 3, 4 and 5 describe new arenas in Songkla and Patani. The Chapters examine in particular social formations, organization, ideologies and the activities of local movements. In summary, the research interest concerns the agency of the movement. Chapter 3 is divided into two parts: the Chapter sketches first a portrait of Thai non-governmental organisations and networks in Songkla and provides second an insight into the dynamics of re-constructing local Islam in the Southeast Asia/Middle East connection. Identity performances in locally-based social movements in Southern Thailand are interpreted in a comparative schema.

Klum 'Rao Rak Songkla'

Locally based groups in Songkla have developed into a lively social movement. Professionals are organized into networks and organizations to have a say in public life. Lawyers, doctors, journalists, academics, teachers, entrepreneurs and civil servants have been organized into business associations, philanthropic foundations, alumni and charities. The campaign for klum rao rak Songkla constitutes a new quality of the public sphere, integrating the Thai Buddhist middle classes. This integration brings together people of various strands and backgrounds from business circles, NGOs, academic circles who have sometimes never cooperated. No wonder then the people's organisation of Songkla Prachakom has to overcome divisions within the movement itself. The 'people's organizations' of Songkla Prachakom has grown dynamically in the late 1990s. Indeed, the core group has had problems adjusting to the fast growth and institutionalization of the networks. As

a result of this growth, the Chamber of Commerce and local government have shown interest in and recognized Songkla Prachakom as a
major platform of public life. Local academic circles have been encouraged by the opportunities of political reform to open Songkla Prachakom for political debates and to prepare their own political careers. In
doing so, they have been helped in no small part, by the accompanying
community media which has been critical of the performance of the
Songkla *baan koet* campaign and is a springboard for popularity, charisma and a career in the political arena (e.g. Chapter 4). The sociocultural
movement, its activities, social organization and its cultural codes are
shown in Table 2.[1]

Table 2. Local Civic Groups: Songkla Prachakom

Communities of practice	Performance	Language	Religion	Media	Organization
Songkla Prachakom	*baan koet* campaign	Thai	Bhudhadhasa	Core radio	Songkla forum, NGOs, wat, political reform

Practices and Activities

During the Learning Festival (*tesagarngarnrienru*) from 9 to 11 March
1996, 24 children completed a large wall painting of Songkla under the
tutelage of four adults. For that purpose, local teachers and artists guided the children to important sites of Songkla, covering the public buildings, the school, the hospital, the Buddhist wat and the mosque, taking
paper and pencils with them. The mural featured a lot of green, modern housing, the main street, Songkla Lake, the fishing, and in the centre of the mural, a bright wat. The artwork was presented to the festival
audience of the festival at Songkla City Hall. The artwork summarizes
well the purpose of the festival: the main purpose of the festival was to
learn about the participants' place of birth (*baan koet*). The people were
urged to rediscover the beauty of their hometown.[2]

The people of Songkla were encouraged to take a break from daily
life, to begin to think about a 'vision' for Songkla, and to exchange new
ideas in this direction. The label 'Learning' Festival has been chosen to
emphasise the role of teaching. As the invitation form to the festival

explains, the access to knowledge is a condition for the ability to participate in, and develop creative thinking for, the making of the modern world. The subtitle of the festival 'Learning Thai ways of life, feeling Thai hearts' (*rienruvitithai, duainuajaithai*) expresses the quest for authenticity.

The festival aimed to raise awareness of Songkla culture in the minds of Songkla's people. Reflection on the landscapes of Songkla and a sensibilization for the consequences of social change were set in motion. This process of reflection was achieved through 'educational games' in which awareness of the place of birth in the face of threats to its integrity was raised. The aim of the festival was to inform the 'people' about Songkla's history; It was also intended to win friends who share an interest in a better society and most significantly, the festival—in a dramatic way—puts local groups on centre stage. Buddhist sermons of the great monk Phra Bhuddhadhasa Bhikku were presented in a radio programme. Buddhism is considered a natural and authoritative protector of the community as well as a social order. The promotion of kao yam Songkla is a nice illustration of the use of symbolism: one pamphlet reads: 'Songkla people like to eat *kao yam* Songkla'.

Local foods are chosen to represent Thai culture, traditions, a nostalgia for the past; kao yam Songkla symbolises—a somewhat essentialist—version of Thainess. Local foods represent authentic Thai culture in the face of social change and the influx of Western lifestyles, e.g. McDonaldization. The new relationship between humans and nature is one of the priorities of non-governmental organisations (NGOs) in Songkla. The commercial exploitation of nature is criticized. Songkla Lake is seen as the lounge of Songkla, as nature is considered the lounge of the *muang*.

Songkla Prachakom and Songkla Forum were initially no more than a loose friendship groups, but developed in the face of potential sponsors into a core group of local intellectuals and a number of quasi-members who can be called upon when the occasion arose.

Youth was thought to have a critical role in the future of the locality. According to Pannipa Sotthibandhu, one of the organizers and managers of Songkla Forum, a profit-minded capitalist culture is at the root of the social ills of modern Thai society. 'As long as people are interested in money making, community-building will not progress.'

Key terms of the public discourse were 'new ideas', 'creative thinking' and 'thoughtful action'. 'Peace' and 'peaceful action' were emphasized. Theravada Buddhism is the only guide and ethic that members should apply to their actions.

The peoples' organization aims for no less than the construction of a new subjectivity, a subjectivity that makes the individuals conscious about themselves, the collective and the environment. Moreover, the individual is asked to begin a process of learning about the community concerns. As a result of togetherness, a world of harmony is to be established.

I have accompanied an organized walk to a temple in Songkla Lake. Guided walks leading to a forest temple in Songkla Lake is associated with reformist Buddhist connotation. The walk is associated with Dhamma Yatra, meaning that spiritual energy is set in motion.

The process of religious awakening is spelled out in rich detail: understanding the walk as a form of Buddhist meditation, the participants learn to concentrate, to breath, to get to know themselves and to reflect on their action. The participants learn to understand their practice as a religious mission. Thus, the Dhamma Yatra walk becomes a religious experience and the participants are enlightened by Buddhist wisdom. Buddhist sermons of the great monk Phra Bhudhadhasa Bhikku are intelligently integrated in the radio programme. Buddhism is considered an authoritative protector of the community as well as social order.

Furthermore, Songkla Prachakom organises seminars. Local intellectuals are encouraged to think about how to contribute to the general interest of the community. For example, professors have been invited to discuss the contribution of religion. Presentations to this seminar covered Buddhism, Christianity and Islam.

The discursive practices of self-organized groups in Songkla borrow from the public discourses of Thai intellectuals and reformist Buddhism. The inspiration for campaigns, festivals and seminars is borrowed from the community culture school (*watthanatham chumchon*), from the teaching of Dr. Prawes Wasi, and from the sermons of Phra Bhudhadhasa Bhikku.

The 'people's organizations' focus a legitimising public discourse on meaningful locality, family and social change.

The people of Songkla are urged to wake up from lethargy and to participate in the activities for the 'common good' of Songkla. The core group mobilises the people of Songkla to join the 'family' of the core group for the sake of baan muang. This discourse endorses the ideas of prominent Thai intellectuals. Among the most prominent is Dr. (*mor*) Prawes Wasi. According to Prawes, Thai people are in a state of 'greed', because the roots and the traditions of Thai people have been left behind. Social problems such as pollution, rural poverty and AIDS plague Thai society. Endorsing the ideas of Mor Prawes, Songkla Forum brings in national discourses in and adopts them to a local level. This popular Thai discourse on Thai values is not limited to Songkla, but influential among intellectuals and NGOs throughout Thailand.[3]

This communitarian discourse on 'Siam in Crisis', the construction of local tradition and 'local wisdom' is popular among Thai academics in contemporary Thailand.[4]

The authors of Songkla Prachakom maintain that the survival of Thai society in an age of globalization depends on reviving local communities. The movement in Songkla is gaining in self-confidence and is also linking up with other cities of Thailand in a network named citynet. Why do people participate in the activities of Songkla Prachakom or Songkla Forum? My informants told me that they are undertaking activities for society, activities that they like to separate from the sphere of home and work. Thus, a motivation for joining includes a desire to do something together with one's peer group, to work on the social reputation and to contribute to the family's name and to receive social recognition from the others. People cannot live without meaning. By joining the activities of the club, members feel that they give their life a meaning to their life. Public space allows for meaningful action.

Spiritual power spreads by worth of mouth and quickly attracts new members. Significantly, the new middle classes perform their discourse on the stage of public life, and, by doing so, reformulate ideas of morality, community and justice. By engaging in this reformulation, the use of reformist Buddhism and officialising discourse, local intellectuals proliferate in the Songkla public sphere.

In 1999, the movement grew rapidly and was at the height of its power and level of activity. The movement was planning the 'greening' of private banking. Commercial banks and corporations are encouraged to assist the ecological recovery and to use funds for that purpose. The private radio station would be transformed into a centre for local media.[5] The core associations of Songkla Prachakom are networking with local leaders in order to assist people in need.

Significantly, the movement has been inspirated to enter the political arena as a consequence of political change in Thailand. Ajaarn Vichai Kanchanasuwon, Aree Rangsiyogit and Supak Inthongkong have used the parent organization of Songkla Prachakom to establish a new organisation on decentralization and political reform. The political efforts of the Thai-Buddhist middle class in Songkla received fresh momentum with the new constitution in 1999. Core leaders aspire to enter the formal political process and to benefit from the opportunities offered by the elections for the new senate. The organization is also is using the platform of Songkla Prachakom to attack power abuse, corruption and patronage, and to put transparency, human rights and personal rights high on the agenda. Therefore, the 'council for political reform' is carrying out a popular campaign that promotes the application of political reform on a local niveau. The leadership seeks intimate relationships with democratic institutions in Bangkok and has invited national leaders such as Anand Panyarachun to Songkla.[6] In personal discussion, the representatives (Ajaarn Vichai, Aree and Supak) of the new organisation and network admit that progress to apply the new laws in Songkla has been slow and has been resisted by the traditional elites. The council for political reform promotes a new vision and is using the media (print media as well as television) to disseminate ideas on clean politics (instead of money politics). While Ajaarn Dr. Vichai, Supak and Aree prepare for political careers,[7] the inability of the organization to change local politics causes increasing frustration and illustrates the impotence of the movement in relationship to traditional elites.[8] The powerlessness sometimes limits the movement to the level of ideas and visions. However, the discourses, cultural images and symbols of Songkla Prachakom are gaining quickly in importance and visibility.

Intellectual Figures and Locations

Pannipa Sotthibandhu is recognised as the most proliferated person in Songkla. Being the daughter of the President of the Prince of Songkla University's Hatyai campus, Pannipa Sotthibandhu has all the credentials to lead civic groups in the Songkla public sphere. Khun Pannipa Sotthibandhu has been a member of Songkla Prachakom's board, the director of Songkla Forum and the chair of the group's community media, including Hatyai Talk (Hatyai Sontana) and private radio stations. She is currently heading an institute for vocational education in Songkla.

Pannipa's evaluation of local Thai society is indicative of the legitimising discourses of Songkla Prachakom's people's organization. Pannipa points out that 30 years of development have violated (*komkün*) Thai society and led to a fast deterioration of Thai culture and Thai ways of life. Pannipa analyses the changes in Thai culture from the angle of the family. She is concerned about changing ways of life in urban areas. Pannipa regrets that young people do not look up to old people. Parents do not have time for the family. People do not know each other, are egoistic and are caught up in consumerism. Transport and communication cause anonymity and pollution. This situation is compared with the good old times. The traditional Thai community is a lively space of communication and tradition (*püntihengchiwit*). The spirit of solidarity and local knowledge was transmitted from one generation to the next. There was rice in the fields, and fish in the canal, an old Thai saying. The nostalgia for the community characterises the approach to the development of the *muang*. The goal is to re-establish some of the community-spirit.

The *muang* is compared to a house. Spaces for the family, children and communication must be established. Pannipa hopes to raise support and awareness by 'enlightenment'. She hopes that the old creativity of local communities can be revived, the spirit of Thai traditional values revived and that the violation of creativity and ideas can be stopped. She hopes to revive communication between father and mother, generations and neighbours. The family is considered to be the cell of a healthy community.

Pannipa directed the 'Learning Festival', initiated Songkla *baan koet* and is heading the private radio programme. Pannipa travels regularly to Bangkok in order to keep in touch and to link up with national democratic institutions and international foundations.

Ajaarn Aree Rangsiyogit is Dean for public relations at the Rajabhat Institute in Songkla. He is a foundation member and the President of Songkla Prachakom. Ajaarn Aree Rangsiyogit worked his way up from a humble background of informal and formal education in Bangkok and Songkla. He holds positions in several institutions of higher education in Songkla.

Ajaarn Aree is a charismatic leader whose help is widely thought. Ajaarn Aree is an intimate consultant to the governor of Songkla who would not ignore him for important decisions. Ajaarn Aree is preparing for a political career and will be a candidate in the forthcoming senator elections. He told me that the Non-Governmental Organisations (NGOs) have to adjust to the modes of Songkla Prachakom, because the NGOs in his opinion are too much biased against the government. He hopes to beat corruption and vote-buying and prepares for a political career. Ajaarn Aree hopes that Songkla Prachakom will organize the political arena in Songkla in such a way that the core group of the local groups has a hand in important political decisions. Ajaarn Aree thinks that the people's organizations have been empowered by the membership of politicians and entrepreneurs and are on their way to challenging traditional society. Thus, Ajaarn Aree is standing for power within the movement. He expects the new members from politics, business and the NGOs to adjust to the new rules. Ajarn Aree is thinking of becoming an independent politician.

Chamnong Raekpinit has organised the farmers in Songkla for many years. He is a graduate from Thammasat University (political sciences) and is based at the Institute for Southern Thai Studies in Songkla.

Chamnong is recognized as a leading figure in the NGO-milieu. He is co-operating with many international donor agencies, among them Miserior, Terre des Hommes and Oxfarm. One of his programmes has been the organization of small-scale credit and saving cooperative in Songkla. Chamnong has been highly successful in raising financial support and in organizing farmers' associations. In addition, Chamnong Raekpinit has good connections with NGOs in Bangkok. He is the person who is mediating between Songkla Prachakom and rural institutions. He is also the person who is mediating between international donor agencies and rural institutions. Thus, Chamnong is coordinating the NGO and peasants networks in upper Southern Thailand.

Chamnong, integrating urban and rural associations, has been approached by many local groups to represent Songkla's interests. Chamnong will comply with this desire and will be a candidate for the coming senator's elections.

Concluding Remarks

Acknowledging the idea of a strategic group, the local group is using cultural tools, the invention of tradition and the transmission of knowledge for public life. The community is edging out and, with performances of public discourses through their own media, provides a forum for communication. Members constitute and reconstitute their identity within the community. They draw on their educational capital to justify their leading role in the affairs of the city and to defend their mission. Thus, they claim access to specialized knowledge and, indeed, refer to a Thai discourse on siwilai. Avoiding a political discourse, action is legitimated through anchoring the community into Thai culture, in tradition and Theravada Buddhism. Buddhism has woken up from its apathy and a more activist Buddhism (of Bhudhadhasa Bhikku) is used. The movement is creating attention in dramaturgical fashion in terms of Goffmanesque theatre society.

Does the Songkla-based movement take the place of a third sector between market and state? The 'club' provides a forum for the organisation and networking of the Thai-Buddhist middle class. The cultural movement presents itself as firmly anchored in Thai culture. Interestingly, it is not the central Thai culture that has been performed in the urban events, but rather, local community culture. Local people are urged to participate in the building of baan muang in Songkla. Although the association does not challenge the legal or political system, the middle class is increasingly able to impose its moral standards on the rest of urban society. From this angle, the club succeeds in an upgrading of the cultural field. The enhancement of the cultural field is strengthening the position of the new middle class. The strategies of the people's organizations in Songkla are processes of local reconstruction, self-awareness and emancipation.

Islamic Chant, Patani, South Thailand.

Local Muslim Society in Patani [9]

With the transformation of the Patani region from being a tributary Malay principality to an ordinary Thai province, local Malays,[10] as a Muslim minority in a Buddhist nation-state, remember the 'good old times', when the Patani sultanate was well known as a 'cradle of Islam', attracting Muslims from the Malay peninsula and far away places. This nostalgia for a lost state seems to characterize in a nutshell the psychological situation of the local Malays, cut off from the Islamic heartland and bound up with the religious cosmology of the Thai nation-state. Remembering the past not only recalls Islamic heritage, but, by implication, involves the ambition to reorganize local Muslim society in Thailand. Related to this claim to cultural autonomy is the claim to possess a history. Thus, the resurgence of Islam in contemporary Southern Thailand is a response to the denial of Malay history in Thailand. The integration of local Muslim society into a global Islamic sphere also results in the active recall of the Patani Islamic locality.[11]

On my visits to Southern Thailand in 1996, 1998 and 1999, I felt a growing Islamic self-awareness in local Malay society. This growing self-awareness had to do with the specific development of the region. A dramatic transformation has been going on in traditional Muslim society for some time, which has certainly led to a breakdown of traditional Islamic institutions. This transformation touches on all domains of Muslim social life. The breakdown of traditional institutions has caused rivalries in local Malay society over the authority to interpret Islam and to shape Muslim cultural spaces. This process was further fuelled by the channelling of the central educational system into the periphery. A new Malay middle-class segment is responding by making use of the Thai as well as the Malay educational system in Malaysia. The educated Malays have been instrumental in establishing an Islamic public sphere that a religious community, social organization and communication network makes possible the negotiation of social space for Muslims in Patani.[12]

The Islamic public sphere, its dynamics and structural change and the application of central concepts and visions in local society have been the subject of anthropological investigation. Students who return from schools in Thailand, Malaysia, South Asia and the Middle East are crucial communicators of Islamic self-awareness. The special relationship between the Islamic public sphere and Islamic movements in Northeast Malaysia must be underlined, because Malays from Southern Thailand have chosen the Malay states of Kelantan and Trengganu as places of political exile. Muslims have to respond to the Thai public sphere as a stage, where Muslim identity and culture have to be performed. They can also be contested and negotiated in the process of realizing performance. So we can only speak here of an Islamic public culture as an appendix to the Thai public culture. This becomes even more obvious if one relates Islamic public culture to the sphere of public education and the different ways in which Islamic education is related to it. Here, we have to ask: 'how does the global form of scriptural

Islam influence the field of local Islam, how do shifts in local Islamic knowledge which have become part of 'global knowledge' influence Islamic practices of the local Malays and how are new Muslim spaces designed in local society?' To answer this body of questions, the claims, visions and utopias of local Malay intellectuals are studied in the light of channelling the global Islamic sphere into the local. For whom and for what purpose is the new religious style and discourse on morality being developed? What does the politicisation of lifestyles and gender relationships mean for the modernisation of local Islam in Southern Thailand? Moreover, the situation in Southern Thailand should, moreover, always be compared with local Islam in neighbouring Kelantan because of the cultural and linguistic affiliation.[13]

Che Man's Vision of the Local Islamic Community in Patani

The most fundamental aspect is thus the increasing power of the Thai nation state and the expansion of Thai modern education. The period during the 1990s was marked by a paradigmatic change towards Islamic institutions. The Muslim minority participated in the national political process.[14] The Muslim political faction Wahdah (Unity) aligned itself with any national political parties who pay attention to Muslim interests. Mr Wan Muhammad Nor Matta, member of the Wahdah and deputy leader of the New Aspiration party (NAP) is serving as elected speaker of the Thai parliament and is President of the National Assembly. Muslim support for the Wahdah faction is increasing in the south and is gaining popularity among Muslims residing in other parts of Thailand.

Over and above the cultural bonds of Southern Thai Muslim society to Saudi-Arabia, and the intruding Thai modernity, a new religious style has taken on form, power and visibility in Patani. Muslim intellectuals take a lead in restructuring Islamic education, ordering everyday life and reworking ideologies about family, gender and race. The saturday sermons of Dr. Isma-ae Lutfi in his pondok some kilometers out on the road to Yala has become a public event that appeals tremendously to Muslim academics and students, and attracts large crowds every week. The scholar and preacher epitomizes a new breed of Muslim intellectuals in Southern Thailand. Lutfi has become something of a media 'star' for his bourgeois clientele: Using the microphone and loudspeakers to reach the crowd, his sermons are recorded on audiotape and can be bought either on the spot or in Muslim shops that specialize in Islamic media and clothes. Lutfi is widely known and respected for his Islamic knowledge, for reciting long passages from the Qur'an and the Hadith in Arabic, and for his networks with Saudi-Arabia where he completed a Ph.D. degree in Shari'a law. By participating in the public sermons, study groups, discussion groups, networks, associations, clubs, and youth groups, I was undertaking research in what I would like to call performance, space, and the making of an Islamic public sphere. This religious style, literate, rule oriented and purist, appears to have a great impact on the university campus, because Malay academics and students seem to be prepared to submit themselves under the pedagogical authority of scholars such as Lutfi. Kraus (1984) has foreseen the development of a strong orthodox Islamic movement in Southern Thailand, which may attract Malays both from rural and urban areas. The process of local Islamic self-awareness has been dubbed 'Islamic resurgence'; yet, what is meant by 'resurgence' is not always clear (cf. Chaiwat 1993). This chapter has the modest aim of exploring some aspects of local Islamic organization at the local level and to put the changing ways of how local Islam is reproduced in relation to globalization.

The most important group among the religious leaders is religious teachers. The practices of religious teachers and their role in the process of the Islamic community in Patani has been discussed by Che Man (1983, 1990a, 1990b). Religious leaders are given positions of status and power in the society. Religious teachers gain status and power through their religious knowledge and teaching. Che Man (ibid.) maintains that religious leaders are treated with respect because they play a leading role in community activities, 'ranging from prayers to festivals'. In most villages,

> "the Imam, Khatib, and Bilal lead the Muslim villagers in their daily prayers in the mosques. Important religious occasions such as Hari Raya, Maulud and other ceremonies to mark special events such as Kenduri on the occasions of marriage, birth and death always involve religious leaders" (Che Man 1990a: 130).

Religious teachers are divided into tok guru and ustaz. Che Man (ibid.) has found that religious teachers were active in the Malay separatist conflicts in the 1970s. As Che Man (ibid.) explains, the religious teachers in Patani society rose to fill the roles left vacant by the raja and their ruling aristocrats who where deposed and dispossessed by Thai authorities. The activities of the religious teachers are not strictly limited to the religion, but operate along socioeconomic and political parameters.

In the following, the writer is concerned with a new generation of urban scholars and with their religious style. The rise of local intellectuals is intertwined with the increasing contacts of local Islam with the Middle East. It appears to me that the new Islamic public sphere is firmly embedded in global modernity.

Che Man notes that Imams are given status and power in the traditional Muslim community. Describing Islamic traditions in Patani, Che Man compares the Islamic community to a big family, using the intimate words 'family' and 'communal life' to describe the key institutions of Muslim social life, the mosque and the pondok. He writes that the relationship between students and teachers and that among the students themselves are as that in a family:

> "Life in a pondok is similar to that in a family. Students live in small individual huts, also called pondok, which are built around a central building where teaching and prayers are conducted. The pondok's objective, apart from teaching religious subjects, is to inculcate a sense of morality based on Islamic principles. Teachers are unconditionally obeyed by students because they are regarded as the students guardians or as members of their family" (Che Man: 1990a: 264).

In the 1990s, the situation of the pondok seem to deteriorate quickly and many pondoks were stricken by poverty. Che Man only mentions in passing the requirements that have been imposed by the Thai bureaucratic system. The material situation of the traditional ulema seems to be more serious than Che Man appears to admit: the moral economy seems to be collapsing as the erosion of the subsistence sector and the need for cash forces Malay peasants into the towns or to Malaysia to seek work. As the region is integrated in much wider national and transnational economic circuits, new consumption patterns develop and change the way of life. For example, Malay pupils may develop more interest in Thai pop concerts and the Manchester United football team than in Qur'an reading groups.

However, in the 1990s, the traditional Imams seemed to lose their grip on the ownership of the Islamic public sphere. The Imams are being replaced by scholars who are inventing different ways of communicating Islamic representations. The restructuring of the pondok has profound implications for the way local Islam is reproduced in Patani.

The new religious specialists are given substantial status and power. The role of the Muslim preachers is greatly enhanced through the Islamic landscapes that are emerging between local societies and that of Petro-Islam. International migrations for higher education sustain the personal networks that feed the Islamic landscapes. The religious style differs from that of the Imam who is respected for mystical qualities. The new religious style is rule-oriented and anti-esoteric. The Imam marks special events such as marriage. The new style is sober and puritanical. The Imam is looking for a mystical relationship. The new style is literalist and Shari'a-oriented.[15]

The urban scholars can capitalize on their Islamic knowledge and transform it into economic capital in turn; weaving patron-client relationships with a bourgeois clientele, the urban scholars are engaged in forms of accumulation. The private character of the Islamic schools makes student fees and donations obligatory and Islamic private schools an attractive enterprises.

Among the traditional Islamic institutions, the mosque is the centre of religious and communal life. In the nineteenth century, these masjids also functioned as schools or universities, within which scholars taught the fundamentals of religion such as Sufi mysticism and languages.

When the institution of the mosque was placed under the authority of the Provincial Council for Islamic Affairs (PCIA) as part of the Thai governmental administrative structure in 1947, it was no longer considered as a private institution. Some 25% of mosques in the region remain unregistered. The formation of a mosque council was an attempt to regulate the activities of the mosque, which became not only the centre for religious activities, but also a meeting place where political issues were articulated. The Kru Se mosque is a case in point. The Kru Se mosque has become a centre of political activities and an important symbol of Muslim identity and social memory in Patani. The activation of the mosque can be interpreted as an effort to re-appropriate the mosque as a private institution and to defuse government interference. The mosque, mosque associations and mosque activities are all experiencing change.

New Styles and International Exchanges

As Antoun (1994) points out, very little attention has been given to migration for higher education, to the interpersonal aspects of migration or to the reactions of migrants to prolonged exposure to alien cultures and to radically different living circumstances (Antoun 1994). The work of Mona Abaza on Indonesian students in Cairo is the exception in that she focuses just on these issues (Abaza 1991b).

The studying experience involves much more than Islamic studies. There is a constant negotiation between local traditions and modern Islam in Cairo. As a result of exposure to Al-Azhar, Abaza has observed an Egyptianization of Malay students in habitus and lifestyle, language, dress and food habits. The students (including Malays from Thailand) build strong transnational networks that seem to be establishing travel routes, networks and milieus between insular Southeast Asia, Cairo and Mecca. Many Patani students have gone abroad to study Islam, particularly in the Middle East.

The diversity of and fierce antagonism between Muslim groups in Patani creates a highly competitive atmosphere. It is the more education-oriented Malay youth who are attracted to the modern preachers whereas the poorly educated respond to the traditional ulema. Prominent members of the leadership and Muslim academics are split between one local group that promotes the internationalisation of Islamic education, the introduction of English, and scholarships to obtain degrees in the Middle East and in the West and other local group that is pulling away from Western education and is pushing for the Islamization of knowledge; this group leans towards the Islamic centre. The ambitious programme of charismatic scriptural leaders to reorganize Islamic education in Patani Muslim society is on the defensive. In such a situation, the institutionalization of a Whahabi, scriptural religious style in an Islamic public sphere, is enhanced through the embeddedness of these leaders in an internationally organized network, providing Lutfi and others with powerful allies and a material base that enhances considerably its stand in this competitive situation. Being equipped with social and material capital, Islamic knowledge and funding, the new Muslim intellectuals stretch out to reorganize Islamic institutions, such as the mosque, the pondok (Islamic school), the Muslim economy and the Islamic media, which they make ample use of. The Islamic institutions are now considered in Table 3 on Muslim social spaces in Patani:

Table 3. Social Spaces for Muslims in Patani

Community of practice	Performance	Language	Religion	Media	Organization
Islamic intellectual culture	Islamic sermon	Melayu, Arabic, Jawi	Islamic reassertion	Islamic media	Mosque, pondok, Madrasah

Personalities, Networks and Locations

The visions, claims and utopias of (selected) Muslim personalities will be examined in the context of specific life biographies, Islamic networks and locations of Muslim intellectuals in the Islamic public sphere. Their social standing in local Muslim society is based on charisma, involvement and responsibility in shaping cultural space for Muslims in Patani. The visions, claims and utopias have to do with the global sphere and inform us, I believe, about the emergence of religious landscapes that channel the global into the local. The subtle differences in Muslim discourses represent competing positions for envisaging the public sphere. This cultural complexity of local Islam gives a picture in which local Islam in Patani is developing at different tangents.

Dr. Hasan Madmarn is a fine academic who, coming from a humble family background, has become a true cosmopolitan and great scholar. Dr. Hasan Madmarn spent many hours with me discussing his role in local Muslim society, his personal history, his involvement and his role as an educator. He characterises himself as an open minded conservative who appreciates values, family ties and local traditions. I chose to include him in the study, because he represents a certain kind of scholar who is dedicated to modernization of Islam, but who considers himself a conservative and a local.

Dr. Hasan Madmarn has become the Director of the College for Islamic Studies which is attached to the Faculty of Humanities at the Prince of Songkla University. From a humble family background in Phatthalung province, Hasan Madmarn describes his parents as pious and committed Muslims who provided their children with a solid Islamic education in the Chana district. His rich description of Islamic education in the Chana district gives a good insight into the Muslim milieu in Thailand.

Hasan Madmarn began his first year at pondok Padang Langa in the years before 1955. He recounts that his tok guru has been very popular among southern Muslim communities: tok guru Abdul Ghani was a young scholar from Kelantan, with excellent training who well versed Arabic. Hasan Madmarn's pondok was geared towards the Madrasah system. Later, he has envisaged a political career, and has been a candidate for local election, although he has not been elected. Dr. Hasan Madmarn holds a doctorate from Temple University in Philadelphia and has learned with Professor Fazlur Rahman in Chicago. Hasan Madmarn's dissertation on the pondoks and Madrasah in Patani not only deals with the process of change, but can also be read as a plea for the modernisation of Islamic education in Patani. Dr. Hasan Madmarn summarises his programme as follows:

> "Muslim religious teachers are aware of the need to carefully adjust from the old system (pondok) into the modern system (Madrasah). That is to say, they require that the Madrasah system be introduced into the Pondok in order to serve the needs of the modern times. At the same time, they demand that the old system of traditional Islamic heritage be retained and taught" (Madmarn 1999: 81ff).

The modernisation and streamlining of local Islam according to global standards is Madmarn's vision. Madmarn aims to harmonize Islamic tradition and Islamic modernity, and urges the new generation to keep and respect the local cultural heritage. Madmarn aims to save the kitab Jawi (traditional Islamic literature) and hopes that the Madrasah system of Patani will be taught along the same lines of those of the Middle Eastern countries.

Dr. Hasan Madmarn believes that the Malay students will have to master the Thai, Malay and Arabic languages to comply with the demands of the Thai government. He would also like to see Muslims from Thailand going to the Middle East in large numbers in order to further their education. In his vision, the pondok is a preparation for higher education in Cairo or Mecca.

While Dr. Hasan Madmarn underlines the historical continuity of Islamic networks connecting Patani with Mecca, Dr. Lutfi would like to establish the Arabic system of Islamic education in Patani. The reformist approach of Dr. Lutfi is clearly influenced by Islamic middle class study groups throughout the southern peninsula (*dakwa*) and clashes, in part, with the traditional ulema whose mystical approach to

God and whose traditional authority has been undermined by scripturalist scholars such as Lutfi. The textual approach to the holy Qur'an
as the only base of authoritative knowledge reflects the transformation
of public Islam from the traditional type of Islam confined to the rural
kampung to one which is led by a new breed of Malays with tertiary education whose direct engagement with the holy texts is based on an Islamic education in Saudi-Arabia, bypassing the received wisdom of the
traditional ulema.

The nomination of Dr. Isma-ae Lutfi as the president of the first
private college of Islamic Studies in Thailand is major step forward in
his grip on power over the public sphere. Orthodox Islam shapes the
curriculum as well as campus life. A Diploma of Theology is offered in
accordance with the guidelines of the Thai Ministry of Education. The
Arabic language is considered the language of the holy texts, and Arabic has become the language of instruction. The emulation of Saudi
standards depended on implementing a rigid separation of gender and
the regimentation and enclosure of the female body.

Hj Wan Muhammad Shaghir Abdullah is the head of the Shaykh
Daud bin Abdullah al-Fatani Foundation in Kuala Lumpur where I visited him. He has chosen political exile in order to re-vitalize the cultural
heritage of classical Islamic works of Patani scholars in the nineteenth
century. Muhammad Shaghir is a grandson of the well-known scholar
Shaykh Daud al-Fatani and showed me the original works of Shaykh
Daud. Muhammad Shaghir runs the foundation to keep the classical
works alive. He is a visiting professor of the Faculty of Islamic Studies
at University Kebangsaan Malaysia and has written commentaries on
the Patani ulema's classical works and of Patani's Islamization in particular. Shaghir has taken his pupils with him to Malaysia. In addition,
he has attracted members of the Malay middle class who aim to study
the classical works of the traditional ulema and who respect Muhammad Shaghir for his knowledge of Islamization in Patani, his acquaint-
ance with the Patani scholars and his knowledge of the history of Islam
in Patani. Muhammad Shaghir has been to Mecca to study the kitab Jawi. He represents the local conservative tradition, and the Kelantan
connection. As a disciple of the Sufi brotherhood, Shaghir is deeply
emotionally deeply involved with the cultural autonomy of Patani,
whose representatives have found their political exile in the federal
states of Kelantan and Trengganu. Muhammad Shaghir is a representative of the classical ulema and asserts that religious leaders also have
a political role in resisting the Siamization of Patani Muslim society.
Whereas Dr. Hasan Madmarn has a decidedly pragmatic attitude to-

wards the Thai state, and Dr. Lutfi asserts himself to be 'a man of peace', Muhammad Shaghir deeply desires the return to or establishment of an Islamic state according to the Kelantan model of the Islamic party.

The Islamic schools are the most important institutions of power; the restructuring of Islamic education is fundamental to the realization of central concepts and visions. Here, the utopias and visions for local Islam are powerful discourses that are applied to the socialization and schooling of Malay youth. The imposed vision not only concerns school and campus life, but also regulates the private sphere and covers all domains of everyday life. Muslim intellectuals in Southern Thailand are looking to the Middle East for the restructuring of Muslim society. The increasing exposure to the Muslim world is reflected not only in images or pictures, travel and fluidity, as post-modernists seem to argue, but also in the making of tight social organization at the local level. Muslim identities are embedded in the construction of Muslim spaces. Muslim intellectuals use religious beliefs and Islamic networks to shape and organize Muslim life in the overlapping domains of family, home, school and mosque. The construction and shaping of Muslim spaces has depended in a large part on the input from a new breed of tertiary-educated Malay Muslim intellectuals. Unlike the traditional tok guru, the Muslim teachers not only provide a religious education, but also operate on different levels of Muslim social and political life. The emergence of charismatic leadership in Southern Thailand has depended in large part on the prestige of educational degrees and international experiences in local Muslim society. Education and international experience are 'written' in the habitus of islamic intellectuals. Hasan Madmarn speaks fluent English and has international contacts in the West. He dresses in Western-style dark suits. He is known as a diplomatic and able intermediary who receives visitors from Malaysia or Indonesia in his house, including visitors from the Ministry of Foreign Affairs. He is also a very able administrator who represents Muslim interests in Thai government agencies. Hasan Madmarn is a local from a Thai-speaking Muslim community in Songkla. Madmarn is converses in Bahasa, but does not speak the local dialect. He has good standing with the traditional ulema.

Dr. Ismail Lutfi has excellent contacts with Saudi-Arabian Islamic organizations. Lutfi speaks fluent Arabic, including Arabic dialects, and is able to declaim long passages from the holy texts and the Shari'a in the Arabic language. Lutfi has a modest lifestyle, wears Arabic white-coloured robes and rejects material comfort or luxury. Lutfi supports the claim of the PAS in neighbouring Malaysia for an Islamic state. Lut-fi is a native of Patani. He converses in Patani Malay with his audiences, reciting in Arabic from the Qur'an.

Muhammad Shaghir is a conservative scholar. He is a local whose knowledge is firmly based in Patani's history. Muhammad Shaghir keeps tight contacts with the Patani ulema, to the Patani Muslim print-ing houses and to Islamic organisations in Malaysia. He considers Siam a colonizer of Patani.

The three schools of thought illustrate different discourses and dif-ferent contexts in which discourses are produced. In addition, they show different visions and utopias for contemporary local modern Muslim society. They are competing political economies of meaning, envisioning in practices and discourses different ways in which Islamic traditions are reproduced. As ideal types, they represent conservative, modern and orthodox approaches to constructing, using and shaping Muslim spaces in a minority situation. The habitus relate to their rela-tionships with the social memory of the past, the embededness in Mus-lim networks and relationships with the Thai bureaucratic polity.

Hasan Madmarn represents a school of thought that strives for the harmonization of the old and the new. Hasan Madmarn looks back to a glorious past. He believes that the authority of the traditional ulema has to be respected and wants to modernize the institutions of Islamic education along the standards of the Middle East. In addition, Hasan Madmarn is putting effort into the idea that Muslims in Thailand ben-efit from cultural citizenship. Hasan Madmarn wants to go through the system to help represent Muslim interests. Ismail Lutfi is the media star of the Islamic public sphere that depends on the charismatic leadership of highly-educated young scholars. Lutfi's scholarship challenges the authority of the traditional ulema. The introduction of a new stock of Islamic knowledge constitutes a rupture with the past. Malay visitors from the Islamic University in Kuala Lumpur told Lutfi that he cannot emulate Medina in Thailand. Lutfi stands for the increasing encapsula-tion of the Malay Muslim community in Thailand; the emerging Malay middle class in Southern Thailand is looking for spiritual support from him. Academics visit him in order to learn. Lutfi stands above ordinary people. Muhammad Shaghir represents the traditional ulema. He has left Southern Thailand; cooperation with the Thai state is not desirable. Muhammad Shaghir aims to revitalise the cultural heritage of his fore-fathers. He does not embrace the new ways of Islamic education which are compromised to the Thai educational system and cannot accept the foreign ideas of scholars like Lutfi. In summary, the orthodox scholars and the modernists vie for ownership of the Islamic public sphere in Patani.

Communicating Islam in the Public Sphere

Senior religious teachers disapprove of frivolous amusements, including music and carnivals. The disapproval of fun-spaces not only marks an internal conflict in the Muslim field, between old and young, but also concerns the socialization of Malay youth into Thai popular culture. The discourse of fun-spaces, entertainment, dance and music works with metaphors of good and bad Muslims and evoked Muslim discourses about the evil worlds in Thai cities, the seduction of sensual pleasures, the world of brothels, discotheques, cafes and karaoke bars. The stigma of Muslim backwardness is, in a psychological and philosophical sense, turned into its opposite: that of the ultimate superiority of the Muslim system of belief.

The label fundamentalism has contributed little to the analysis of social change in Muslim society. The development of an alternative perspective focuses on the re-negotiation of Muslim identity, life planning and life aspirations. This negotiation of identity involves the emergence of a poly-tactic identity and stresses the ways in which Muslims participate and build their life projects in Thai modernity. My argument is that this kind of negotiation is increasingly realized in the space of the Islamic public sphere.

Advances in transport and communication have facilitated the emergence of transnational Muslim spaces and Islamic networks, and intensified religious exchange which has put the Muslim minority in Thailand in much closer contact with the Muslim world. The experience of the Muslim pilgrimage and the sheer presence of Islamic images in Southern Thailand creates imagined communities well beyond the boundaries of the nation-state. The imagined communities beyond the boundaries of the Thai nation-state are also supported by the proliferation of Islamic community media. Islamic media are those media that are produced by Muslims for Muslims. The post-modern condition in Patani is supplemented by media such as books, audiotapes and videotapes. Through the media, local Muslims can access Islamic images from Mecca and Bosnia. Satellite television allows for the reception of Malaysian television. Accordingly, radio stations in Malaysia broadcast to Southern Thailand's border provinces. The media cross international boundaries and spread the message of pan-Islamic unity.[16]

Globalization seems to have added a new dimension to Muslim travellers (Eickelman and Piscatori 1990). The willingness of the local Muslims to move has increased greatly. Among the lower classes, Muslims from Patani earn their livelihood in the rice-fields of neighbouring Malaysia. Among the middle classes, more parents send their children to study at Islamic Universities in Cairo. In short, more Patani Muslims are on the move. This increasing mobility has led to the creation of transnational networks of Muslims from Thailand, Malaysia and Indonesia. Transnational organization at the Thailand-Malaysian border has intensified. Malay Muslims from Malaysia and Thailand meet regularly in study groups. There are du-ah missionaries who receive monthly salaries and allowances from different Islamic call centres in the Middle East (Che Man 1990a).

The Muslim teachers disposing of authorized Islamic knowledge become brokers who mediate between local and global cultural forms. The Muslim teachers become gatekeepers for Saudi Arabian culture and it is through them that local Muslims hope to get access to Islamic knowledge and to participate in Islamic modernity.

Urban scholars are given confidence and responsibility in managing Islamic economics. Urban scholars manage saving and credit funds and use the skills of Muslim graduates.

Thus, religious leaders use knowledge/power systems to engage in Muslim forms of accumulation, and to occupy positions in the local arena. The social organization is akin to the theory of strategic groups: the religious teachers weave strong power structures through nets of kinship and inter-marriage, personal networks and pondoks.

The Ustaz imposes educational techniques and new religious styles on a local society that has its own indigenous tradition of Islamic knowledge. In fact, the emergence of a new public sphere has fundamental implications for the Muslim field. The new Muslim discourse clashes with the traditional ulema whose source of identity and authority is undermined. The scriptural movement has attempted to purify local Islam of pre-Islamic, Hindu or animistic beliefs and contents in Muslim rituals and festivities. Furthermore, the zeal of purifying Islam involves the eradication of fun-spaces, such as music, dance and carnival. The Muslim field is not static or monolithic. Here, the Muslim public sphere is conceptualised as a contested space in which young and old people and traditional and modern ulema vie for cultural supremacy.

Leading Voices of Public Islam

Class formation in Malay society is decisive for the construction of an Islamic public culture and for its ethos. Participation in the activities of the public sphere requires forms of literacy from speakers and receptors. The Muslim orthodox teachers are successful in communicating their programme to Malay academics and students, to entrepreneurs and civil servants and soldiers. Why is it so? The staging of Islam as public virtue provides an alternative ideological consciousness to constructions of Thai national identity and appeals to the aspirations of young adults to join global networks of religious exchange. The feeling of global solidarity with the Islamic block in Saudi-Arabia liberates the Patani Malays from feelings of isolation, loneliness, and estrangement. In participating in the activities of the public sphere, the members succeed in constructing alternative sources of cultural citizenship, to build self-esteem. As Abaza argues: "The (imagined) Arab traditions have been recreated and reinvented in Southeast Asia to fit with the constraints and pressures of modernity which emerging middle classes are undergoing" (Abaza 1991a).

Likewise, the habitii of Muslim intellectuals are nourished by symbols and manners of Arabic dress, *Halal* food and Arabic dialect language. The new members of the *Dakwa* groups emulate the symbols to display and signal their membership of Islamic modernity. Islamic lifestyles are displayed and indeed celebrated in the public sphere. The orthodox public sphere provides the space where cultural identity can be realised. The scriptural movement uses religious beliefs in order to make and shape Muslim cultural spaces (e.g. Chaiwat 1993).

Public Islam provides a powerful religious tool in the hands of Muslim teachers to mobilise and to discipline members. When the language of religion gains ground in public discourse, religious specialists acquire the power of definition of public norms. The performance of public sermons is a critical practice in staging and communicating Islam to the audiences. Social life is like a play in which roles are distributed and in which people engage in symbolic interaction. The mosque, the Islamic school, the home become the stage at different levels of society.

The performance of Islam in the Islamic public sphere and the communication of Islamic representations develops in tandem with the growth of a cultural market.

Education is the key to the social reproduction of Muslim spaces. The College of Islamic Studies, which is located on the campus of the Prince of Songkla University, has developed into a centre of intellectual exchange for the Muslim community.

The making of Muslim spaces organises at the delicate threshold between home, school and mosque, between the domain of the family and larger social organizations. The emergence of an Islamic landscape that is gaining in strength in Southern Thailand through transnational networks in the Muslim world has drastically changed gender relations. The Islamic schools are the most important agents of socialisation into gender roles. A lot of pressure is exercised here from the teacher and the older students to adjust to dress codes.

Ong's (1995) analysis on gender relations in modern Malay life reveals how the discourses of the Islamic resurgence have incited and intensified concerns about female sex, space and actions, and how concerns about women's bodies are used to redraw the boundaries between Muslims and Non-Muslims. Ong (1995) argues that educated women found the dakwa call so appealing because as wives and mothers, Malay women can adjust to pressures of moral uncertainty and find Islam a system which guide them through a period of rapid change. She concludes that women become implicit allies of dakwa organisations to create patriarchal domination in both public and private spheres. However, my empirical data support the thesis that Muslim women did organise in alternative networks and that women make themselves visible in the construction of new Muslim spaces, such as associations, study groups, mass prayers, consumer groups, Qur'an reading groups and Muslim women's networks more general.

I had the fortune to accompany committed female journalists and to participate in the making of news, columns, features and debates in local Muslim society. Superficially, the women may submit to patriarchal relationships, but the same women find the authority of Islam attractive for developing female spaces in which their activities in the public sphere are recognised for their religious purpose. Through dress codes and dakwa practices, Malay women communicate strong boundaries to non-Muslims, especially Buddhists. Arab symbols are recreated in order to cope with the pressures and tensions which the emerging middle classes are undergoing. The community of practice nourishes and supplies Muslim spaces with their own media/culture/knowledge material for. Local media thus play a crucial role in the negotiation of ethnic and religious identities.

Concluding Remarks

A new breed of Middle Eastern-educated scholars has taken the initiative in weaving prestige, contesting culture and realizing Muslim identity. In order to assert and make their identity visible, the educated Muslim middle class endorses the scriptural Muslim discourse and the visions, claims and utopias that are affiliated with the rapid transformation of the Patani Muslim locality. This transformation is marked by the increasing cultural bonds between Patani and Saudi Arabia, the increasing integration into the Thai political system and increasing cross-border Muslim public life. The analysis of the particular relationship between teacher and disciple reveals the modes of social reconstruction of local educational forms and Islamic knowledge as well as the great appeal that the educational techniques and shifts in Islamic knowledge have for the Malay middle class in Thailand. Islamic education is a crucial resource for Muslim identity in Thailand. The communication of Islam as a social virtue is carried out in an Islamic public sphere which has gained quickly in strength and power in the 1990s. The establishment of a public culture is instrumental to the growth and strength of the charismatic leadership of Muslim intellectuals in Southern Thailand. The anthropology of performance, culture and space is particularly well suited to explain the formation of collective identity and the changing ways in which local Islam is reproduced in local society.[17]

The transformation of the person occurs at several levels. Socialisation under the new educational techniques is certainly the most influential instrument of producing docile bodies. The young students coming from the kampung adjust to the rules of the pondok. Many women have to trade their pastel-coloured or flowered clothes for long robes and headcloth. Enrolment in the educational institution also requires correct demeanour and conduct. Some students aspire to become model students, to keep the rules or to spy on the activities of their fellow students. Starrett (1998) argues that today's Islamic assertion is rooted in new ways of thinking about Islam that are based on the market, the media and the school. New styles of religious education, based on moral indoctrination, together with new forms of communication have changed the way the Islamic tradition is reproduced. Educational techniques together with the commodification and mediatization of Islam result in a rapid Islamisation of public spaces.

Now, what are the new ways of thinking about Islam in Patani? The transformation of local Muslim society is occurring in a perspective of crisis. Indicators for this crisis are the rapid diminution and irrelevance of many rural pondoks, the erosion of the subsistence sector and blunt poverty and the marginalization of Malays in Thailand. The extension of the Thai state into the periphery, the rapid expansion of capitalist markets and the expansion of the Thai educational sector all fly into the face of Malay nationalism in Patani. In this situation, the Islamic networks with Malaysia, Egypt and Saudi Arabia have produced a new breed of tertiary-educated Malays who assume a key role in negotiating social spaces in education, gender relations, Muslim social life and in re-imagining the Patani locality.[18] In the new Muslim spaces, Muslim identity is not coupled to Malay ethnic identity.

4

Community Media and
the Politics of Nostalgia

What little attention has been paid to the media in Thailand has been concentrated on the institutionalized Thai mass media, such as television and broadcasting. Little attention has been paid to the media in Thailand at a local level, whereas the massive presence and fast spread of the media in Thai late modernity calls for ethnographic data on the media in Thai public culture and everyday life.

As Hamilton notes, it is impossible to understand the media and cultural expression in capitalist Southeast Asia without recognizing the central role of the state (Hamilton 1992). Thailand too, has seen the mass media as a primary mechanism for national development and ideological conformity. Through a variety of formal and semiformal mechanisms, and through the structures of ownership and control, most institutionalized media is under direct government control. Stations and air-time are subsequently leased to private enterprise, but the overall control lies squarely within the state.

The efficacy of state control over the media may provide its own negations. The readings of the audience may not conform to the intention of the broadcasters. As Hamilton says,

> "in Thailand what is not said, the resounding silences, can open up fissures, through which an unofficial discourse is constructed and rapidly circulated" (Hamilton 1991).

In addition, modern mass media has the potential to escape from the clutches of the state. The fast spread of new media technologies into the periphery transgresses national boundaries and slips beyond the reach of the clumsy bureaucracies charged with the task of surveillance and intervention. As Hamilton has observed, the appetite has been whetted, but hardly satisfied by the available viewing diet.

In Thailand, the proliferation of media reform is at the heart of the development of a public sphere. The media anthropologist Ubonrat argues that the media reform parallels the democratic and cultural trans-formation of contemporary Thai society (Ubonrat 1999). In this transformation, different social forces struggle for media space in or-der to set their agenda for public attention. Ubonrat argues that the media expansion does not signify a greater degree of freedom for peas-ants or workers. Rather, it demonstrates the growing strength of the middle class, which is in a better position to capture the media space. The appropriation of the community media in the boundaries of the club in Southern Thailand illustrates this process empirically, as out-lined by Ubonrat (1999). It is argued that both media reform in the po-litical domain and media expansion within the framework of globalization and mass consumption enable movements such as Song-kla Prachakom or scriptural Islam to capture media spaces.

With the presence of the media, the way of life is not the same. The spread of media technologies to nearly every corner of Thailand has enabled small producers to use small-scale media for their own purpos-es. Community media is small-scale, private media, such as radio, vid-eo, film, print media, brochures, pamphlets and slide-shows. Community media is emerging in the space between the state and glo-balization. The state was an enthusiastic promoter, using the media for its propaganda interests. However, national efforts to use the mass me-dia for hegemonic ideologies and images, however, are increasingly be-ing subverted by global, as well as local, images.

Making media is crucial for the construction and shaping of the public sphere. Community media is media technology that is appropri-ated in the local context. As shown in previous chapters, the education-al core groups of the respective social movements supply themselves with their own culture/knowledge material. Community media fits in the construction and shaping of the public sphere. The task is to put the community media in existent forms of popular communication. Thus, analysis of the community media should not be separated from everyday life and from public life. Community media plays a very im-portant role in the articulation of interests in the public sphere, for stra-tegic action, for the discursive construction of the group's programmes, and for the construction of cultural identity. Thus, com-munity media can be defined as small-scale, private media technologies that allow small producers to address a very specific and limited local audience. Community media can be used to transport very efficiently and very rapidly political, cultural and religious contents and to con-tribute to the spread of cultural identity. Thus, the Media are important in the formation of cultural identities. The argument is that far from replacing face-to-face relationships and personal networks, media gives a new dimension to these networks and allows for a more efficient and more performative articulation and expression of collective identities. The increasing importance of the public sphere in Southern Thailand gives new space for small producers whose production and distribution of small-scale media lies at the heart of the mobilization of the movement. Competing community media are summarised and compared in Table 4 within the framework of social movement:

Table 4. Community Media Compared

Community media	Content	Religion	Language	Location
Core radio, pamphlets, brochures, journals, slides	*baan koet* campaign, education on political reform	Than Bhud-dhadhasa (homepage www.suan-mokkh.org)	Southern Thai dialect	Bangkok, Songkla
Islamic Media, tapes, books, video-tape	Social vir-tue, Islamic lifestyle	Scriptualist Islam	Patani Melayu dia-lect, Jawi	Malaysia, Kelantan
Chinese, video, televi-sion	Chinese rit-ual, Chinese identity	Kwan Im cult	Thai	Bangkok, Taiwan, Sin-gapore

At stake is the post-modern debate on public culture: who has the authority to speak in an increasingly diversified media landscape? From a comparative perspective, this Thai example illustrates the centrality of community media in the struggle for public opinion, and the efforts in developing public space in a period of cultural and political transformation. Furthermore, it provides a case study on the uses of community media as a means of articulation in the public space. As argued in previous chapters, the public space does not develop from scratch, but has to be carefully constituted by local groups. The systematic use of media technologies is part of strategic action for the improvement of the chances of intervention in the public space.

Hamilton, by taking from the beginning the point of view of the active audience, showed how people choose, combine, and circulate media representations and other cultural forms in their everyday communicative interactions and in doing so produce meaning in everyday life worlds. She has also pointed to the creative use and subversive readings of the Thai mass media. Hamilton has started a media project that is conceived around the question of cults and ritual move-

ments, where she looks to the role of different media in the construction of cultural identity. In her study on Thai media[1], Hamilton
discusses the striking impact of video in Thailand. In Thailand, the vid-
eocassette recorder (VCR) has penetrated the country with amazing rapidity: in cities and provincial towns, the VCR is, one way or another,
available to everyone. Hamilton describes how people arrange to du-
plicate pirated masters by the tens of thousand. More significantly for
the purpose of my paper is the appropriation of video for local and private cultural activities, such as the taping of a Chinese spirit ceremony
(Hamilton 1989). The edited version of the tape was duplicated and
copies were sent to the medium's relatives all over the country, whereby her fame as a medium was spread, encouraging people from distant
parts to attend her possession ceremonies or come for healing. Here,
the media spread knowledge about Chinese cults and rituals throughout the country. As Hamilton notes, the creative use of small-scale, private media allows for the rapid circulation of cultural meaning
throughout the country.

Using a flexible framework of borderlands, I saw the whole zone of
the Southern peninsula as a borderland and I was interested in exploring the many borderlines and practices of distinction of the Thai Buddhists in the upper South and the Malay Muslims in the lower South,
including lines that are based on identity and popular culture. The complexity of the media in Southern Thailand reflects the significance and
variety of media in a growing cultural market. We can distinguish three,
overlapping media-spheres: A national media sphere (early evening
TV), a global media sphere (global telenovelas, videos, video-discs and
music CD's, cinema) and a local-born narrative media landscape, drama and *Manora* dance and *Nang Talung* Shadow Puppet theatre. Each
media sphere has its own dynamics that cannot be discussed in full detail.

Ordinary people have been extremely keen and creative consumers
of media. The presence of the media in everyday life, especially video-
taping, recording was overwhelming. As for community media, the important step is not to concentrate either on the reader or on the producer, but to realize the interaction between the two. The researcher
observes the levels of production and consumption at the same time.
This is especially so for community media. While media anthropology
has focused on the practices of media consumption, the community
media helps to overcome the producer/reception paradigm. The members of Songkla Prachakom and the members of scriptural Islam are
not only subversive consumers of hegemonic media texts, but are also
involved in the production and reading of the community media's images. In making media, the people are themselves involved in the struc-

ture of the public world. The character of the community media is such that communication can develop outside of the national media sphere of the state.

Making Waves: Core Radio and other Media in the People Love Songkla Campaign

Songkla Talk is the centre-piece of Core radio. The directors of Songkla Forum have employed skilled journalists to design a sophisticated entertainment programme. The radio programme is roughly organized in information, education and entertainment sessions. Songkla Talk informs about its agenda, its campaign and invites people to its public events. The largest share of its programme is reserved for educational purposes. Taking up the ideology of Songkla Prachakom, Songkla Talk surveys the state of society and politics, discusses social problems that plague Songkla's people, and invites potential local intellectuals to become active:

> "Most *Ajaarns* are content in doing teaching and administration work. That's all. Some of them are are teaching and are doing research. That's the minority. Only a few think about their responsibility about society for society" (an academic from Taksin University speaking for a seminar organized by Songkla Forum).

The radio programme of 'Core radio' takes the listener as an implicit member into the atmosphere of the club. The audience is invited to participate in the making of public opinion and public life through the media. The programme managers' language is one of cultural intimacy, taking the audiences into the 'family' as an intimate relative. Articulation through its own media enables the club culture to create cultural spaces and to create a communication of the core group, the producers, and the people of Songkla. The calls that urge people to wake up and to join the activities of the core group for a better society are a pattern of a discourse aiming to mobilize segments of the educated urban middle classes. Core radio as a private local radio station creates new media spaces, presenting itself as an alternative to the conventional mass media, which, in the opinion of the cultural managers are driven by commercial interests.

The striking feature of Songkla Talk is its growing popularity and influence. Core radio provides the audiences with a new type of media experience. The proximity of producers and audiences allows the audiences to be part of the radio session and to make its voice heard. The relationship between the radio and the audience is much more intimate than for other programmes.

Core radio is a community-supported non-commercial public radio station. The non-commercial nature is stressed by the cultural managers of Core radio and has contributed in no small part to its success. In addition, the marketing of local tradition and local identity as well as the regular and frequent audience makes Core radio an extremely attractive radio programme on which to advertise. Local enterprises play on the spirit of locality to promote their products and services and cleverly fit into the intimate atmosphere of the listener club. The enormous success and high legitimization have enabled the organizer to expand the radio programme to other stations, such as the station at the local university campus, and it now comprises five local stations, including public and educational stations. The managers of the many organizations of Songkla Forum have become respectable and even charismatic people who are invited to join talk shows by the primary television channel 11 which is managed by the Ministry of Education and is a non-commercial channel without advertising. Core radio moved to the FM band, and now broadcasts everyday in the morning for 30 minutes and on week-ends for 2 hours. The long Sunday seesions are able to catch the local audiences and to try experiments, such as including children's voices into the family programme.

Songkla Prachakom has discovered the local media. The core group is constructing a centre for local media in Songkla that is supposed to play a more active role in public life. Private radio is the very core of this media sphere. The centre is supposed to hold a library, slide and videoshows, public displays and public performances. The centre of local media is integrated in the idea of a community centre (*Bürgerhaus*), which is supposed to become a material space for the people.

The radio creates a clientele that is bound together through the experience of participating in Songkla Talk–either as a speaker or as a listener. Local media is embedded in the framework of the dynamics of the Thai public sphere in Songkla. Songkla Talk helps local organizations to stage the public events, to prepare, mobilize and document the Songkla Learning Festival, guided walks, seminars and campaigns. Local media is put in a relationship with other existent forms of communication, such as folk songs, drama, theatre, and Buddhist sermons and Buddhist meditation. Buddhism has a tremendous influence on the discourse of public speeches: 'new ideas' are emphasised, creative thinking and thoughtful action. So are peace and mindful action. Buddhist ethics are communicated as authoritative guides that members are encouraged to apply to their everyday life. The association is legitimizing activities by borrowing from the words of Bhudhadhasa, and from his charisma. Core radio is targeting a mid-to upper-income group and the programming of local cultural arts and music is an integral part of the radio station's image.

The community radio of Songkla Prachakom has seen great expansion in recent years. With the growing legitimacy and power of the movement at hand, the group is now broadcasting in some five radio stations, including the university-based radio stations. The radio has contributed to the increasing visibility of the Thai's campaign in the public sphere and to the recruitment of new members.

Islamic Media in the Patani Islamic Resurgence

The performance of Islamist religious intellectuals is itself a media event. The people and followers of these Muslim personalities wait for the media stars in the packed mosque, in front of the mosque or in *pondoks*. Ismail Lutfi tours the towns of Naratiwat, Yala and Pattani for his public presentations. His recitation and interpretation of Islamic texts is recorded on audio-tapes and filmed. The tapes of Lutfi are available for sale in the *pondoks* together with videocassettes, pamphlets and books. The crowds acquire collections of Lutfi's sermons on tape which are then routinized in everyday life. Islamic media is crucial to the nourishment of a Muslim milieu that supplies itself with religious material. Listening to Islamic audiotapes of famous Muslim preachers together with family members or friends, the followers continue the relationship of the teacher with the media.

The audiotapes are cultural tools in the improvement of the self. Islamic media, audiotapes of religious leaders, books and magazines help Malay youth with questions of life-planning and orientation in Thailand. The audiotapes are imported from Malaysia and are sold in a new type of shop in Patani that specializes in Islamic commodities, media and clothes. The shop caters to Malay popular demand: both video images of Mecca and the veil are available in the shops which are managed by nephews of the old nobility in Patani. The Muslim commodities represent Arabic imagined traditions that are recreated by the educated Malays to cope with the pressures of Thai modernity they are undergoing.[2]

Islamic Guidance Post is a national Islamic monthly newspaper published in Bangkok in the Thai language. *Islamic Guidance Post* has developed into a leading forum of public opinion for the Muslim minority in Thailand. The *Post* is opening a media space for intellectual debate and cultural identity. In the Letters to the Editor section, the readership is debating with the managers of the *Post*. This section provides a vital platform for debates on Islam in Thailand.

The *Islamic Guidance Post* changed its format in the early 1980s to a monthly newsmagazine and evolved into its current format which includes newsprint quality photographs, colours and glossy inserts. The *Post's* format was also standardized at this time. It was divided into sections, with a primary section on national news, especially as it relates to the Muslim community, another on news from around the Muslim world, a multipage feature report on some important aspect of Thai politics in Southern Thailand, a few columns and regular features. The international news takes readers to the Muslim world, especially to the Middle East. Images of the Middle East are channelled into local Muslim society, so marginal to the heartland of Islam. Like Muslim media in many parts of the world, the *Post* blends moral and religious language directly into its reporting. What distinguishes the *Post* is that it presents its appeals in a language that is accessible, clear and focused on essentials. The *Post* also features critical essays, opinion columns and political interventions. The multi-page report on Southern Thailand discusses Muslim minority interests in Thailand and reviews Thai policies in a critical light. The *Post* thus wants to become a people's tribune, where Thai development programmes are discussed critically in supplements, for example the Indonesia, Malaysia, Thailand growth triangle. The editors want to make the government accountable for its policies and to involve the Thai bureaucracy into a dialogue. The *Post's* editors have a clear strategy of marketing the *Post* to middle-class, educated Muslims in Bangkok and Southern Thailand. The limited circulation makes the *Post* a community medium for the Muslim minority in Thailand.

I had the good fortune to accompany some dedicated journalists writing for the *Post* and other Thai print media. The journalists are integrated into closely-knit networks that allow for communication between producer and audiences.[3] The face-to-face relationships and many personal connections make the *Post* a community medium in which Muslim identity is represented. It is interesting to note that the *Post* addresses the Muslims as Muslims and not as Malays.

Islamic media is part of a much larger transformation of local Muslim society in Patani. New members of the Islamic public sphere aim to demonstrate to become good Muslim. The application of habitual codes confines the realization of the Muslim self to public Islam. Global codes of lifestyles are channelled into the local by means of Islamic networks and media. Clothing becomes a contested space where Muslim identity in Thailand is negotiated and serves as a social language in within which an individual can redefine his or her social position in local Muslim society; Islamic media such as audiotapes from charismatic Muslim preachers helps in this transformation of the self. Yet, the Islamic public sphere can only be conceptualized as an appendix to the Thai public sphere. Thus, Malay students, for example, may turn not only to Islamic media, but combine Islamic media with a large variety of Thai media. This tactical combination of media allows the Malay students to have multiple identities. Thus, the combination of local media characterizes hybrid identity among the Malay youth who are constantly switching codes between the Islamic and Thai public sphere. Doing so, Malay students may adopt to the codes of life that are promoted by Muslim intellectuals, but also counter hegemonic images either by Thai or Islamic media.

Community Media and Media Spaces Compared

The very creative use of local, small-scale media in the emergent public spheres has been emphasized. People at the local level have discovered the crucial role of the media in the public sphere. The growing cultural market and the fast spread of media and media technologies allow small producers to use local media for the club, which initiates feedback processes between producers and audiences. Local media is embedded and should be conceptualized in larger spaces and plays a key role in the mobilization of new members in the club.

The city becomes a stage on which actors perform public culture. As in Goffman's tales, urban life is like a play in which roles are distributed and in which people engage in symbolic interaction. Morals matter in the discourses of the educators. The media plays a large part in the spread of knowledge about them. The focus on codes of life is conspicuous in the Islamic as well as the Thai public sphere. Through the media, the so-called private spheres are debated in the public sphere and lifestyles are made visible and public. Through the media, legitimizing discourses of religious ethics are publicised. Media discourses are working with dichotomies, distinguishing 'ignorant' and 'responsible' citizen, 'good' and 'bad' Muslims, 'heaven' and 'hell' social worlds, and so on.

The social organization is a striking feature of the community media spaces. Moral leadership is provided by religious teachers, academics and scholars, forming the core group. The media managers are making use of very high officializing resources to mobilise, to discipline and 'educate' the audiences.

The relationship between the educators and their bourgeois clientele is ambivalent: media technologies are used to pinpoint loyalties.

The reader, however, may combine very different sorts of media and choose more than one loyalty, in part reaffirm and resist the pedagogical authority of the community media.

The media becomes the spring-board for political careers in the public sphere. Thus, leadership personalities of Songkla Prachakom also become media stars, moderators in podium discussions, whose name and voice becomes popular through specific radio programmes. Thus, key personalities in the movement develop ambitions to pursue political careers. Community media helps sustain and popularise political programmes. The style is such that the movement presents as a viable alternative to the government and an indispensable partner for planning Songkla's future.

On the other hand, a new breed of Middle East-educated scholars have become the media-stars and role-models of the Islamic public sphere. Especially audio-tapes help to popularize preachers whose names are recognized and regarded with awe in Muslim everyday life. Consumers in shops selling Islamic media ask for and request the audio-tapes of certain leaders from Malaysia, such as Nik Aziz Nik Mat. Media stars develop specific styles of recitation for which they are well known.[4]

The community media is firmly embedded in the local and the global. Far to little attention has been paid to the appropriation of local media which has developed in parallel to global mediascapes and has expanded and diversified in the past decade. The marketing of the community media depends on closely-knit local networks. Constituting an important interface between the local and the global, community media makes use of global flows, yet, plays an extremely important role in the construction of locality and local identity. The middle class nostalgia for 'home' and the 'place of birth' is apparent in many activities of Songkla Prachakom, such as in guided walks or in the exhibition of old photographs. Locality, however is put in a broader perspective of global recognition of local cultural inclinations. The researcher cannot escape the local when framing the media in national and global contexts.

The ideology of the Thai state is challenged in the South in indirect and symbolic ways. The local media does not confront the Thai state in explicit words. However, the appropriation and creative use puts the community media beyond the control of the state. Local groups take the initiative from the local state. Community media is very important in the creation of spaces for cultural, religious and ethnic identity. But they are political in the sense that it contests the official ideology of the state which, in turn, so heavily depends on the national, government mass media. It is likely that efforts by the state to maintain control over what people see are being undermined by the facilities provided by the technology itself, and by the indigenous determination of local people to get the kind of media environment they want. In addition, small-scale community media overlaps with other indigenous forms of communication, such as religious ritual or political communication, and can be successfully appropriated by local groups, spreading alternative identities. Media consumers are now able to choose between national television news, print media, radio, global images, satellite, cable, video, and the community media, which caters for a very specific and active audience.

This, community media should be seen and studied in the larger context of public culture and in terms of the relationship of these new forms of communication with local cultural resources and the dynamic spread of locality and tradition. Community media is on the borderline between the performance of local culture and the broadcasting of the same culture. As Lindsay (1997) says, private radio in particular appears to be securing for itself a strong niche for itself, with ever more segmented programming within its local community focus: the paper has focused on only a few examples of community media, yet the resource is there for the study of language usage, radio as an oral tradition, globalization, performance and sociopolitical change in the community. Much scholarly attention has been given to print media and television, but community media seems to have been largely ignored. Yet, like regional cultural identity, it is there, all around, in Southeast Asia.[5]

The Rise of Mediated Publicness in Southern Thailand

According to some sociologists of the media, the rise of mediated publicness introduces new forms of action and interaction and new forms of social relationships and displaces traditional forms of publicness that have been based on face-to-face relationships and on a shared locality. It is argued that the mass media creates a situation in which some individuals produce symbolic forms for others who are not physically present, whereas others are involved primarily in receiving symbolic forms produced by others to whom they cannot respond, but with whom they can form bonds of friendship, affection, or loyalty. The following argument aims to correct this basic assumption on the role of the media in the modernization of society.

The media and new forms of communication in Southern Thailand have not displaced traditional forms of publicness. Face-to-face relationships have not ceased to exist. Rather, the use of communication media transforms the organization of social life in a fundamental way, creating new forms of exercising power. Since the development of print and especially the electronic media, struggles for recognition have increasingly become constituted as struggles for visibility. The Thai Buddhist movement has appropriated the radio to address very specific symbolic clues to a very specific audience. Doing so, the community media has complemented the face-to-face networks and has not displaced them. Community media such as Core radio has neatly established itself in a space in-between the oral tradition and the national and global mass media. The public sphere has not disappeared through the negative influence of the media. In Southern Thailand, we observe a process in which the middle class in Songkla as well as in Pattani makes itself heard through radio programmes, videos, tapes, cassettes, brochures and pamphlets. Using new media technologies, such as the tape or the video, the movements have based themselves on face-to-face relationships. Further, although the movements are able to use the media as very efficient vehicles of transporting symbolic contents to many other parts of Thailand and the world, the community media does not transcend the shared local sphere, but celebrates it. This, again, strengthens the power of the local groups that have used community media. For processes of the change of societies through media and globalization, it is pertinent not only to look at the reception of global media and its incorporation, but to the appropriation of media technologies in the construction of the public sphere.

Social Memory and the Politics of Authenticity

Maurice Halbwachs is one social theorist to have devoted systematic attention to the ways in which memory is constructed socially, particularly in his two important works 'Les cadres sociaux de la mémoire' (1952) and 'La mémoire collective' (1950). Therein, he argued that it is through their membership of a social group that individuals are able to acquire, localize and recall their memories. As Connerton notes (1989: 37), Halbwachs explicitly rejected the separation of the two questions: how does the individual and, how does society preserve and rediscover memory? Thus, Halbwachs (1950: 36) writes,

> "Every recollection, however personal it may be, even that of events of which we alone where the witnesses, even that of thoughts and sentiments that remain unexpressed, exists in relationship with a whole ensemble of notions which many others possess: with persons, places, dates, words, forms of language,

that is to say with the whole material and moral life of the societies of which we are part or of which we have been part."

Halbwachs demonstrated that the idea of an individual memory is an abstraction and that social memory is always collective memory. He maintains that our memories are located within the mental and material spaces of the group. He was convinced that

> "even individual memory is structured through social frameworks, and, all the more, that collective memory is not a metaphor but a social reality transmitted and sustained by the conscious efforts and institutions of the group" (Halbwachs 1950: 36).

Halbwachs showed how different social segments, each with a different past, will have different memories attached to the different mental landmarks characteristic of the group in question. The social segments of the middle class, organized in communities of memory, will have different memories, and are involved in the active appropriation of the past.

Halbwachs, even though he makes the idea of collective memory central to his inquiry, only hints at the crucial question of how social memory emerges, and how these collective memories are passed on within the same social group. The purpose of this chapter is to do this, that is, to illustrate the formation of political pasts in the context of strategic groups.

The Politics of Remembrance

In Chang's words (1996), 'an interpretative power exists in the process of constructing collective memory into social solidarity.' Memory from her point of view plays a crucial role in creating a we-sentiment, a world of reciprocity. Thus, social solidarity is rooted in memory; memory is a meaningful resource and solidarity can be evoked by participating in ceremonial activities.[6]

Accordingly, the transformation of the memorial framework implies the constructed history of a dominant group, but allows for the freedom of the individual to choose between different communities of memory, and the convergence of the autobiographical memory and the collective memory as a result.

As Chang (1996: 60) says, this implies central question regarding constructed history and the shaping of the public arena: 'who selects the different historical contents and interprets them? What is the relationship between the constructed history and the other repressed memories?'.

This relates very much to the questions which I identified as central to the shaping of public arenas and communities of practice, namely the ownership of the public sphere and the authority to speak. To explore these questions, consider the strategies that will be used by any dominant group to strengthen its cultural or political hegemony and repress the other memories within any given society at the same time, strategies of 'organized remembrance' and 'organised forgetting'. Chang (1996: 61) writes; 'obviously the bringing into play of power relations does not simply imply a construction of history, it is rather the attempt to maintain the authority by such kind of interpreted history'.

Thus, the practice of recalling the past is an attempt to shape cultural spaces. The reconstructed history provides the meaningful material for the social construction of the communal spaces, the flesh and the contents of these spaces.

The problem with his sociology of memory is that Halbwachs says little of how images of the past and recollected knowledge of the past are sustained and conveyed by social groups. In a Foucauldian manner, we are interested in the techniques by which pasts are re-enacted, appropriated and by which cultural spaces they are shaped. The emphasis is switching to the political manipulations of the past and not only the historical reconstruction. Looking to the practices of re-enacting the past by which images of the past are conveyed and sustained, in particular, opens a perspective on the relationships of power, of domination and resistance, by which interpretations of history are designed, imposed and contested, by which either complementary or oppositional versions of the past are demonstrated within the context of the communities of memory in their ritual performances.

The Politics of Remembering and Forgetting

Communities of Practice is a sub-theme of identity politics. The associations are forms of class sociability, which allow original forms of communication and, importantly, utopias and visions. The middle classes are the producers, and, with the help of their own media, the articulators of collective identity.

The aggressive promotion of tourism in Thailand has transformed the landscapes and memorial sites of Southern Thailand in tourist maps and commercialized tourist attractions. Southern Thailand, which is considered a sensitive region in terms of national security, has been discovered and marketed in the southern-most axis of the tourist trade. In a context of rapid modernization and urban change, a nostalgia and general quest for authenticity is flourishing in Southern Thailand.

The re-imagining of Southern Thailand and the extensive changes in the subjectivities are taking place in a larger context in which the region is transformed by modernization processes and in which Thailand partakes in cultural globalizations. The positions of East and West, of Westernization, Islamicization and Reformist Buddhism are all facets of a global reality that is increasingly manifest in the region.

Southern Thailand's history is becoming part of a passionate discourse on its cultural heritage. In the politics of selective remembering and forgetting, middle-class agents become keen archaeologists, historians and architects of collective identities. I would like to argue that the appropriations of partial histories are a component of the 'high' cultural productions of knowledge. I would like to show how social memory is incorporated and used in the practices and discursive strategies of the communities of practice. Social memory is cultural capital that is returned in the social arena on various levels of social action. Social memory forms an important part in the assertion of identity in an attempt to shape cultural spaces and is itself a discursive construct of the strategies of selfhood—on the individual and communal level.

Social Memory

Connerton (1989: 2) notes that our experiences of the present depend upon our knowledge of the past, and that our images of the past commonly serve to legitimate a present social order.

A social order requires shared memories:

> "It is an implicit rule that participants in any social order must presuppose a shared memory. To the extent that their memories of a society's past diverge, to that extent its members can share neither experiences nor assumptions" (Connerton 1989: 3).

Images of the past legitimate the social order. The legitimization of the past is problematic in Thailand. Social memory, sustained in commemorative ceremonies, thus legitimizes or questions such a social order. Connerton (1989) argues that images of the past and recollected knowledge of the past are conveyed and sustained by performances.

Furthermore, he points to the manifold ways a society remembers, through gestures, acts and bodily performance.

Taking up the notion of the performative memory, I shall explore the remembering of the past through incorporated practices, as Connerton suggests, and look at the performance of commemorative ceremonies in the public arena. Shared memory in Southern Thailand is very problematic. At the same time, memory seems central in the making of a society and in producing or challenging the social order.

Social memory as a meaningful resource has entered everyday discourses in a moral economy of symbolic goods. Furthermore, the appropriation of history is part of a collective identity that is developed in the communities of practice, here communities of memory. Social memory plays a role in the mobilization of members and provides important material for the construction of shared identity. The presentation of Southern Thailand's history forms part of the stocked knowledge of the educated. The presenters are conscious of the sensitive nature of local history.

Traditions are reinvented as part of a spectacle in which the meaning of locality is negotiated.

The discursive formations are not to be separated from the political stake. The appropriation of regional history and its partial demonstration is confronting the Thai-ization campaign of the state and the important role that the history of mapping, including cultural mapping, plays for the self-understanding of the nation-state. In any society, there are different theatres of society.

However, social memory is a meaningful resource in the globalization processes. Local history becomes a concern of the communities at a time, when the *lieux de memoires*, the places of remembrance, are the subject of the tourist gaze (e.g. Chaiwat 1993).

Tourism is an important dimension of market expansion and of the social transformation in general. Tourism is also a golden opportunity for the representation of Southern Thailand by larger state agencies, such as the National Identity Board and the Tourist Authority of Thailand (TAT). Theatres of remembrance are rearticulated in the frame of cross-border tourism from Malaysia and Singapore. The spirals of tourism contribute in no small part to putting memory on the agenda of the public sphere.

In the following, practices of remembrance and forgetting, especially from the communities of memory, are interpreted as techniques for producing locality. From the outset, locality is reinvented and reimagined in the complex relationships of the communities with the state.

Memory work is not a passive receptacle, but instead a process of active restructuring, in which elements may be retained, reordered or surpressed (Fentresss/Wickham 1992). As Appadurai (1995) points out, the perception of locality has undergone fundamental changes: the media, in particular, has transformed the meaning of locality by creating complex images of distance, self and other and social transformation Southern Thailand is better described as a site in which complex historical processes come into conjunction with global processes that link such sites together. Appadurai (1995) has described these sites as a global structure for the continuous flow of images and ideologies. Social memory has entered the language of cultural politics.

The efforts of the state to control the conservation of the cultural heritage, the aggressive promotion of tourism, and the competing theatres of memory, create complex conditions for the production and reproduction of locality. Constitutive narratives are persistently retold among the groups. An exploration of the theatres of memory always includes individual or collective interactions either with the state or transnational localities, translocalities. Thus, the renegotiations of memory is a battle that touches museums, travel and heritage.

Theatres of Memory

Social memory also includes the cultural productions of Chinese and Malay communities of practice, producing complementary or oppositional discourses on the past. Social memory involves speaking for a culture and of defining the contents of Thai Culture or Islamic Culture. In these authorized interpretations of the past, *lieux de memoire* are associated with versions of history that form the basis for narratives, legends and stories. The narratives of the imagined past provide important discursive constructs in the public culture. Social memory is likely to be found in commemorative ceremonies. Connerton's (1989) argument is that performative memory is bodily. There is an aspect of social memory that has been neglected: bodily social memory. Performative memory is more widespread in bodily practices. In the theatres of memory, the re-enactment is of cardinal importance in the shaping of communal memory.

Connerton's argument can be readily applied to the case of Southern Thailand. Table 5 illustrates the politics and re-enactment of the past in spaces of identity.

Table 5. Performative Memory Compared

Communities of memory	The Imagined past	Commemorative ceremonies	Bodily practic, habitual memory	Identity markers, identity emblems	Re-enactment of the past
Thai professionals	*baan koet*, community culture	Urban event, exposition, blessing	Merit Making (*Tambun*)	Local foods, Southern Thai dress	Prince of Songkla, Luang Por Tuad Saints cult
Islamic Scholar	Lost state, cradle of Islam	Public lecture, oath	Prayer, Ascetic Lifestyle	Veil, arabic dress, Kru Se, mosque, Sultanate's palace	Haji Sulong martyr
Chinese Entrepreneur	Chinese Settlers	Festival, Documentation, Curse	Vegetarianism	Lim Gor Niew Shrine	Kwan Im cult, Lim Gor Niew Saints cult

Symbols from rural worlds (local foods, Southern Thai peasant clothes, folkloric elements) are used in the urban performative culture to support the invention of a local identity and a Southern 'Thai way of life'. In addition, symbols of Theravada Buddhism, nature and political heroes underline the efforts of the 'people's organizations' to create affection and sympathy for the Songkla locality. The history of the *muang* was visualized in the exposition of old photos of Songkla town, showing the old houses, dress and family images, etc. The saints cult of Luang Por Tuad is to be found in the performative memory. Luang Por Tuad is remembered for his magical powers. Stories about him are told and retold in Southern Thailand.

The re-enactment of the Islamic locality is very important for local strategies of Muslim self-awareness in Patani. The re-enactment of the great past has an important psychological dimension for the Malay Diaspora in Southern Thailand. Here, what is being remembered can counter the history that has been, consciously or unconsciously, forgotten. The common history of the Patani and Kelantan *ulema* is embedded in the South-South dimension: The *kitab Jawi* of Shaykh Daud al-Fatani have been printed in Cairo and Mecca and are used widely in the Islamic heartland (Madmarn 1999). The Patani *ulema* and their classical works on *kitab Jawi*, like those of Shaykh Daud al-Fatani forge the past reputation of Patani as a cradle of Islam. In the context of Muslim self-awareness in Patani, Islamic networks with the Middle East and the neighbouring Malay provinces of Kelantan and Trengganu are being revived. The suffering of the Malays in Thailand is epitomized by the remembering of the martyr Haji Sulong who rebelled against hyper-nationalism and was murdered by Thai police.[7] The legend of Lim Gor Niew and the temple cult is an important aspect of Sino-Muslim relations in the South. The unfinished Kru Se mosque has become a place of worship for the Malay community, symbolizing the ordeal of the Muslim minority in Thailand.

The southern coastal Chinese possessed a very distinctive local culture compared with Chinese elsewhere. Hamilton (1999: 10-11), when attending a ritual of Chinese in Yala (of transporting the gods, spirit mediumship and spirit possession), saw a performance of an elaborated series of dances:

> "Wearing costumes remniscent of Imperial China, with painted faces and using clab-sticks for rhythm, this group danced in and around the temple in the evening and again in the morning as the gods were being roused to come down to earth. At the end a long narrative was read out over the loudspeaker, remembering the history of the Southern coastal Chinese" (Hamilton 1999: 10-11).

The spread of accompanying media has helped greatly to the processes of these practices into a space of public culture. The revival of Chinese identity is greatly helped by thousands of visitors from Malaysia, Singapore and, lately, from Taiwan.

In summary, there is a deep historical layer of Thai, Chinese and Malay rituals. Practices of remembering and forgetting contribute greatly in the construction of cultural images. The politics of the past forge a particular Southern identity. Whereas the Thai practices of memory are thus associated with political forms of state power (epitomized by Prince of Songkla, Prem Tinsulanond, Chuan Leekpai), and the Chinese practices of memory arise from the particular history of Chinese settlers (and myths), the Malay memory is concerned with the repression of Malay history.

The performative memory varies rhetoric styles in bringing the past into the present and the future. Among the most influential styles are the blessing, the oath and the curse. The blessing of Phra Bhudhadhasa is not merely a good wish, but brings merit and fortune in the hands of the people's organizations. The oath is a powerful reminder that the Muslims are not going to tolerate the ongoing suppression of speaking about history in public. The name of Haji Sulong, in particular, is put into this context. In contrast, the Lim Gor Niew curse has grown louder in recent years as a result of the growing presence of Chinese in Southern Thailand from Bangkok, Malaysia, Singapore and Taiwan.[8]

The re-enactment of the past in bodily practices characterizes the everyday politics of constructing culture through lifestyles. Bodily practices and more formalized rituals are both material to the performance of social memory in the communities of practice.[9]

Thus, dress is one of the most visible practice of distinction and demonstration of a lifestyle and a highly visible expression of identity.[10] The visual modification makes dress performative. The example of Southern Thailand provides material on the process in which bodily practices, such as dress, are made public.

People in Southern Thailand are making conscious choices when selecting dress. In the life-worlds of the communities of memory, traditional dress comes back onto centre-stage. Through a self-imposed dress code, the members are anxious to conserve their traditions, which are sedimented in the body.

Therefore, both commemorative ceremonies and bodily practices therefore contain a measure of insurance against the process of cumulative questioning entailed in all discursive practices. This is the source of their importance and persistence as mnemonic systems. Every group, then, will entrust to bodily automatisms the values and categories which they are most anxious to conserve. They will know how well the past can be kept in mind by habitual memory sedimented in the body. Clothing is a strong identity marker in the micropolitics, which visibly situates the wearer in a political context. Clothing, like bodily practices in general, point explicitly to the imagined past and is an identity emblem that is performed in the context of the communities of memory.

Whereas dress is the most visible bodily practice of performing social memory, cuisine can also be used in the re-enactment of an imagined past and invented tradition. In the communities of memory, traditional dress and local foods are actively promoted. Members of the communities are encouraged to express a collective memory and shared identity through dress and taste. Cultural festivals of the Thais, Chinese and Malays highlight 'traditional' clothes and bodily practices. The bodily practices are social memories in which the knowledge of the past can be stored.

Dress practices in the public spaces do not reflect everydaylife; rather, dress enhances the performative statement of cultural identity.

The (Southern) Thai dress, combining peasant and Thai aristocratic styles, affectedly help create feelings of belonging in the performance. The traditional dress adds to (and contrasts with) Western, global clothing. In contrast, the Islamic dress sets the Malays apart from the Thai majority. Muslim women play a crucial role in maintaining ethnic symbols, such as clothing and language and minimize interaction with outsiders. In addition, women strongly oppose intermarriage (Chavivun 1980). Muslim habitual practices (veiling) play a crucial role in bringing in new gender arrangements in the frame of the South-South dimension. Chinese variations that are put on for festive occasions include white clothes to express bodily renunciation (for the vegetarian festivals in Trang and Phuket) and colourful costumes of Imperial China to enhance Chineseness.

Thus, dress as a code is woven into the identity politics in Southern Thailand. In this sense, dress-codes are a significant part of the cultural productions. The invention of a 'traditional' dress by Southern entrepreneurs illustrates that businessmen are prepared to show solidarity in order to resist competition from the national centre, Bangkok.

The dynamics of language belong to the bodily practices and habits by which performative memory is communicated. The memory is also stored in names. In Thailand, minorities have to adopt Thai names in order to fit into the model of the Thai nation-state. The adoption of Thai names is a relic from the colonial past. Thus, Malay academics use Muslim synonyms and restrict the use of Thai names to the official sphere. The new name does not necessarily correspond to the old Malay name, but may correspond to a new self-confidence of orthodox Muslims. The psychological significance of naming should not be underestimated. In contrast, the Chinese have no problem in using Thai names. However, the use of Chinese names is common.

The official version of the past is challenged within the communities of memory, which use their own symbols and languages.[11] Thus, in the Muslim public sphere and in the *pondok*, the Patani Malay dialect is spoken, and it comes as no surprise that the Islamic values that differ substantially from the official version, in that different hierarchies and rules are taught, are associated with the Malay dialect, with Arabic, and with the Jawi script.

Thus, just as the Central Thai dialect is the medium of the official past, Malay and Jawi is the medium of the Islamic past. Particular Chinese biographies, in which the Chinese dialect informs about the migrant's origin, are told and retold in oral history.

Some Chinese rediscover the biography of their parents in the Thai language. The documentation of the Khunanurak family shows that this rediscovery of the Chinese past is complimentary to that of the

Thai nation. This book situates the Chinese community in relationship to the Thai state and the Thai royalty. The documentation is about the genealogy of Chinese ancestors. This important documentation shows the assimilation into a Thai political system, their affiliation with the Queen, with Theravada Buddhism, and the Thai state. It nicely illustrates the particular development of the Chinese in Thailand and the South. In this documentation, the Chinese past is beautifully revived and presented to a Thai-Chinese speaking audience.[12]

In summary, language is a medium of communicating memory. What emerges is not one collective memory, but a plurality of social memories that is taught and re-enacted in Thai, Malay or Chinese languages and dialects. The language, together with dress and food, becomes important sites for negotiating cultural identity and contesting social order. This politics of language, which language is used on which occasion, is very closely linked with the assertion of identity and assertion of an imagined past. The Chinese or Malays may speak Thai fluently, but they will continue to practise their own languages within their own communities of memory and their lifeworlds (including their educational institutions). They may switch languages according to the situation and the context to express their place within plural cultures or to demonstrate loyalty/resistance, complementary visions of history (the Chinese)/oppositional versions (the Malays). Thus, bodily practices, clothing and languages are important forms of distinction, in which a political past can be highlighted.

The Curse, the Blessing and the Oath

As Connerton (1989) writes, the performativeness of ritual is partly a matter of utterance. Among the verbal utterances most commonly encountered in rites are curses, blessings and oaths:

> "A curse seeks to bring its object under the sway of its power; once pronounced a curse continues to consign its object to the fate it has summoned up and is thought to continue in effect until its potency is exhausted. A blessing is no mere pious wish; it is understood to allocate fortune's gifts by the employment of words. And like the curse and the blessing, the oath is an automatically effective power-word which ... dedicates the swearer to this power" (Connerton 1989: 58).

Using the example of the sudden death of a young Muslim convert, Nishii (1996) shows the conflictual appropriation of social memory as the families attempt to impose their funeral on the dead body of the young convert. This body of the young convert emerges as a contested symbolisation of social struggle over competing cultural systems. Nishii (1996) has given a vivid picture of the social processes in which social memory emerge.

Taking up Nishii's idea that social memory is a process in which different ways of remembering contest, I shall explain the ways in which social memory is created and, indeed, demonstrated in the communities of practice and used in their partial interpretations of history.

The Past Cannot Be Forgotten

In Southern Thailand, practices of remembering are concerned with the management of emotions, because history is a highly emotional affair. Hatred is a spontaneous emotion that emerges as a reaction to concrete experience of discrimination or ignorance. Hatred can also be directed and manipulated through organized performances.

The remembering of the past has a specific aim: a subjective view of the past allows a claim on cultural space. The recalling of the cradle of Islam provides an opportunity for a growing self-confidence of the Muslims, united in the expanding public sphere of High Islam. The perception of marginality and despair can be transformed into centrality and pride. The sultanate, the palace and trade re-emerge in rich colours and the kingdom of Langkasuka is evoked in paintings of greatness. The centrality of the Muslims is supported by claims of being a cradle of Islam with a history of Islamic teaching and learning.[13] Patani is said to be a place where pious Muslims come from Champa, from Malaya and from other directions to learn in the known *pondoks* of Patani. The cradle image points to the cardinal importance of education in the Muslim communal space.

The recalling of an autonomous history involves semi-secret organizations and the secret mapping of southern landscapes by the Malays. Without a museum of their own, the Malays are able to name and label the many places, grounds and cemeteries. The construction of their own world, their own past is a technique of zoning the physical space around their emotional needs. The Islamization of the past seems a major project realized by Muslim religious leaders, transporting the past into the present.

The Islamic calendar contained only two festivals: the pilgrimage, and feasting in Ramadan.[14] Both rituals have been incorporated into the Muslim public sphere. Travel agencies in Pattani, Yala and Narati-wat increasingly organize the pilgrimage. The pilgrimage is a highlight

in the Muslim media, in the *Islamic Guidance Post* and allows for extensive media coverage on radio and television. Feasting during Ramadan
is a period during which the religious is intensive and during which explicit historical reference are made. The Islamic heritage is re-enacted
in commemorative speeches as well as public lectures, in documentation (in book form), in the Islamic media and in the work of voluntary
foundations. The foundation called Haji Sulong Foundation explicitly
remembers the resistance of Muslim leaders to the Siamization policy
of the military Thai government. In this way, remembrance of charismatic religious figures is combined with current Islamic charity.

The Chinese community dominating economic life also takes care
to preserve the Chinese cultural heritage. In the 1980s, and into the
1990s, the Chinese New Year has become a tourist event. The boost
of the Chinese New Year in Thailand is due in no small way to the ever-
growing flow of Chinese tourists. In the mingling of Chinese Thai cultural spaces, the nurturing of the Chinese heritage in Thailand, Chinese
urban symbols in Southern Thailand, and the promotion of Chinese
festivals in Thai tourism, Chinese social spaces, or ethnoscapes,
emerge, in which the Southeast Asian Diaspora remembers the legends
of Chinese settlements on the harbours of Southeast Asia. The remembrance of Captain China and the Chinese include military strife. The
Chinese have lent a helping hand in a symbiosis with Thai noble families to defeat Malay revolts against Thai occupation. The photos on the
walls of the Khunanurak family home show the symbiosis of the royal
family with Chinese families. This symbiosis strongly symbolizes the
historic alliance of the Chinese and the Thai state. In this scenario, the
Muslims are perceived as a 'fanatic' mob, which has to be controlled.
As Connerton (1989) notes, the performativeness of ritual is partly a
matter of utterance: the recurrent utterance of curses, blessings and
oaths.[15]

The Production of Locality and the Thai State

The attempt of the state to control the conservation of the cultural heritage, the promotion of tourism by quasi-governmental organizations
such as the TAT, and the performances of memory by the communities create complex conditions for the production and reproduction of
locality, in which ties of remembrance weave together various circulating populations that belong in one sense to the nation-state, but are
what Appadurai (1995) calls translocalities. As he explains, translocalities and transnational communities whose solidarity is produced by
known and shared memories are at odds with the need of the nation-

state to regulate public life and public remembrance in the sense that the transnational communities of memory produce contexts of alterations (spatial, social, and technical) that do not meet the spatial standardisation of the nation-state.

Forgetting is as socially structured as is the process of remembering. Thus, the practice of remembering the past is always an action of re-interpreting and remaking the past within the present. In the process of reworking the past, narratives emerge that nest in the discourses on place and more particularly on the present and future of the locality.

Lovell (1998) notes that belonging is a way of remembering and of constructing a collective memory of place, but that such constructions are always contestable. Her concept of locality and belonging explores how collective memory, ethnicity and a sense of longing for the past can fuse in the construction of locality. Belonging may be instrumental in the construction of collective memory surrounding place. Locality and belonging are defined and moulded by memories of belonging to particular landscapes.

Narratives of the past provide important building material for the construction and enactment of particular landscapes. Thus, the selective choice of some building materials and the rejection of others is part of the reconstruction of an imagined community. In the case of Southern Thailand, locality can be recreated through the memory of its existence in the past. Thus, the memory is conductive to the forging of social bonds and contributes in no small part to a structure of feeling, to solidarity. The memorialization of space mobilises people, and represents an attempt to assert a particular identity through interpretation of history. The communities of memory create remembered and imagined pasts and spaces, which can be used as a symbol of other, often political claims. The geographical boundaries, by which cultural territories may emerge, can be called mental maps. The appropriation of history takes place within the framework of the communities of practice that are involved in a constant effort of mapping Southern Thailand anew.

The historical heritage of Southern Thailand constitutes such a contested locality, in which mobilized feelings of belonging express more political claims and assertions in the social transformation of the region. Appadurai (1995) has argued that the multiple forms of rituals, labelling and spatial demarcations, which are easily overlooked by anthropologists, could be interpreted as techniques for the zoning, and production, of locality.

Southern Thailand as a Discursive Construct

Social memory is constitutive for the formation of discourses on Southern Thailand and the perception of Southern Thailand in Thailand and in Malaysia. Southern Thailand's mapping splits into the lower and upper body of Southern Thailand. Lower Southern Thailand is regarded as a problem region and a trouble maker. National security is put high on the agenda. Administration is carried out more tightly. The five provinces of the lower body are called the five border provinces. The border provinces are focus of a special development programme that is protected by the royal family. The institutional commemoration can silence alternative memories of the past. In the emerging public arenas, the discursive construction of the past is highly politicized, negotiated and contested. The dominant discourse of the state is a constant reminder to the different communities that they build their politics of the past always in relationship with the state. The theatres of memory, their commemorative ceremonies and their daily routines are integrated into the ongoing negotiation of Southern Thai identities. The politics of the past are in no way lasting memories stored up in history, but are always revoked and manipulated within social struggles in the present. Thus, the hatred, which the recalling and, indeed, performance, of the past in mass tourism, provokes, illustrates the management of emotions that the manipulation of the past involves in the current social transformation of the region. Social memory is one of the social fields emerging in which the ownership of the public sphere is at stake. The claim on the past is also a signal of demonstrating a presence in public spaces in the present social order. The performative social memory is surely a very important dimension of the design of the autonomous communal spaces that have been established under the lead of the educated middle classes.

Border Stories 3

5

Morals Matter: Cultural Politics Compared

A look at the discursive practices of the cultural movements in Southern Thailand reveals fascinating parallels. Both movements take their
main inspiration from religion. Local intellectuals in Songkla take their
main inspiration from Buddhism. Leading religious leaders in Patani
draw on Islam. Most interestingly, the teachings of Phra Bhudhadhasa
and orthodox Islamic intellectualism are both reform-minded, rational
versions of their religious systems and seek a radical re-interpretation
of their religious doctrine, using them as the main tool for the mobilization of followers. The spirituality of reformist religion gives additional weight to the seminars, lectures and campaigns of the movements.
Religion legitimizes actions and provides a code for creating 'high culture'. Both movements give emphasis to the educational role of local
intellectuals: the core group of Songkla Prachakom is comprised of academics and teachers; religious scholars lead the Islamic movement.

Both movements are integrated into global systems of ideology,
representation and reference. Here, the most important difference has
to be pointed out. The locally-based Songkla movement is closely integrated into networks of civic groups on a national scale, especially with
democratic associations and religious circles in Bangkok. The Islamic
religious movement is orientated towards Malaysia and the Middle
East.

As in Goffman's tales, urban life is like a play in which roles are distributed and in which people engage in symbolic interaction. Codes
emerge and are brought to the centre stage, not least with the media.
Individuals in schools, colleges and universities are highly respected
figures in the Songkla public sphere. In my interviews, teachers stated
that they have a great responsibility for the welfare of society. Some
teachers are well known for their seniority, are sought after for their
opinions in decision making, and take a guiding role in community affairs. As one teacher explained to me, he sees his social responsibility
as not limited to the affairs of the school. Rather, he believes that he is

teaching his pupils to be responsible members of society. He elaborates that teachers are in a special position to guarantee a just and harmonious social order.

Local Islamic scholars have a mission from God to disseminate the message of the Prophet to the population. Because of their religious authority, Islamic scholars are widely recognized as spiritual leaders. Islam is understood to be a comprehensive body of knowledge, which should be applied to all spheres of life. The representatives of an orthodox Islam intellectualism are legitimized to lead through the *ijazaz* from their shaykhs in Saudi Arabia.

Therefore, knowledge, competence and education qualify local intellectuals to take a lead in the spiritual movements. In other words, knowledge is contrasted with ignorance. From this perspective, the 'common people' should seek the wise guidance of the educated. What are the key terms in the movements religious discourses?

Bhudhadhasas's political writings emphasise the importance of *Dhammik* or moral leadership based on the *dasarajadhamma* or ten Buddhist principles of moral leadership. Jackson has shown that Bhudhadhasa's reinterpretation of doctrine leans more towards authoritarianism than democracy and towards a strong moral leader, who is able to lead the collective (Jackson 1989). Within this context, Chamlong Srimuang was mentioned as one such a strong moral leader by members of the Songkla core group.

With regard to orthodox Islam intellectualism, moral leadership is provided by the Imam. The concept of the clerical leadership in the *ulema*, also rests on the strong moral leader, who is giving the right interpretation of Islam and also leans more towards authoritarianism. Nik Aziz Nik Mat, the political leader of the Malaysian Islamic Party (PAS), serves as model for the Malay Muslims on the Thai side.

Apart from their different religious affiliations, Chamlong Srimuang and Nik Aziz Nik Mat have some leadership qualities in common. Both are strong, even authoritarian leaders who rely on moral concepts. The presentation of both leaders in the public sphere is remarkable. Both leaders demonstrate a frugal lifestyle. This lifestyle involves the suppression of any human desire and includes taboos on alcohol and sexual desire between men and women.

'Correct' and authoritative social conduct is one of the great themes of the movements: serving as a model of correct conduct, the leadership styles of Chamlong and Nik Aziz Nik Mat have a strong anti-consumerist and anti-Western undertone. The style with which both leaders represent themselves in public, in a Buddhist temple, or for the

Friday prayer in Khota Baru, visually support and lend credibility to the political discourses, legitimating their political action. While neither Chamlong nor Nik Aziz are physically present in Southern Thailand, they provide role models for the movements.

This moral conduct in daily life is contrasted with contemporary Thai society which is interpreted as being in a state of crisis, a crisis that is seen foremost as a moral crisis. The subjects of social inequality and rural poverty are conspicuously absent in these discourses. Instead, cultural subjects such as family, love and sexuality, as well as apparently trivial issues in everyday life, such as food and dress, are brought to the centre stage.

I want to argue that the educated middle classes participate in cultural politics in an attempt to shape cultural spaces. Clearly, an explicit attack on the political or economic system is avoided in the movement's discourses. Rather, the leading local figures present themselves as spiritual leaders in moral matters.

Tradition, Modernity and Globalization

Tradition is a crucial category in the discourse of both Songkla's movement and of orthodox Islam.

Songkla Forum aims to develop an affinity of Songkla's citizens with the 'home' (*baan*). A romantic image is attached to the notion of 'belonging'. An exhibition of old photos, advertising for local Kao Yam Songkla foods, a changing relationship with nature, a guided walk and a painting of Songkla by Songkla's children are activities that aim to raise an awareness of the authentic locality: the old photos are shown to remember the good old times, at a time when the old buildings are disappearing. Local foods are appreciated, when global fast-food chains have altered the eating habits of Songkla's people.

Within the activities of the community of practice, a reconstruction of the locality is taking place. 'Locality' is put in a broader perspective of global recognition of local cultural inclinations. The significance and relevance of the locality is enhanced through its incorporation into world spaces.

Songkla Forum and Songkla Prachakom are using new technologies of media and communication in order to put their campaign high on the agenda. Being a local movement, the core group establishes links with Thai NGOs in Bangkok, within the Thai City-Net and even with international organizations abroad. Songkla Prachakom is borrowing from the discourses of Thai intellectuals, reformist monks and global NGOs. Terminologies such as community, environment, development and good governance have entered the discourse of the local movement. The community of practice can be compared with a globalized 'green' movement in which the apparent paradox of conservation and renewal is a marker of a new political culture. These global, alternative concepts are channelled into the local. Being a local movement that is situated in a globalizing context, Songkla Prachakom has a self-understanding of being firmly based in a Thai culture.

Within orthodox Islam intellectualism, the reconstruction of the locality is also taking shape. The reconstruction of Islam in a local context is incorporating the locality into world spaces. Islamic institutions establish Islamic networks to the Islamic world, in particular with Malaysia, Indonesia, Egypt and Saudi-Arabia.

It seems to me that an understanding of the concept of Thai culture is crucial for an understanding of the cultural dynamics in Southern Thailand. The following examples are presented to illustrate that the invention of tradition is not a remainder from the past, but an expression of global modernities.

Cultural Politics Compared

The social construction of communal spaces is crucial for the new power of the middle class. In focusing on the new quality of public life, I aimed to show the strategies by which the ethnic segments of the new middle class aim to bring middle class issues into the public realm.

In this light, the public sphere is not open for all and does not correspond to the ideal type of civil society. Rather, the public is a project that increasingly has to match the rationales of the culture market.

In this sense, first of all, the public sphere has to be invented. Moreover, the emerging public arenas are highly contested social spaces. Thus, I am looking to the ways, in which publicness is socially produced.

Publicness counts, because the middle class is more and more able to initiate a dynamic on its own; the players aim to consolidate their grip on the public. The Southern Thai case enriches the problematic of the constitution and transformation of the public sphere: In the public sphere, the middle class is enabled to communicate their legitimate model of behaviour. To put it bluntly, the institutionalization of the life conduct is taking place in the public sphere.

The efforts of disciplining members require specific forms of social organization and, as we will see, original forms of leadership and guidance. The movements are led by an intellectual elite, through whose brokerage people are disciplined as members of a larger, translocal community. The Islamic public sphere is dominated by religious leaders who successfully mediate religious norms. The hierarchical relationship in the public sphere reflects the tight management and regulation of the religious staff. In fact, the Islamic public sphere does not allow participation in the making of public life: laic members are mere audiences of the religious 'media stars'. Still, there is a communication system between leaders teachers, and followers students. The religious leaders are crucial to the Islamic public spheres; the mobilization of the middle class depends on their charismatic leadership.

As for the civil movement, the campaigns are carefully planned and staged by a small circle of core members. This circle is comprised of highly-educated people, occupying influential positions in the educational field. In the process of opening up the communicative space, this circle and network of local 'intellectuals' communicates the issues-ethical, environmental and political, to the audience. The movement is loosely organized, and comprises a cluster of circles, networks and groups, which are loosely tied to each other and mobilised in the urban 'Event'. In the process of the institutionalization of the movement in associations, such as Songkla Forum, the Council of Political Reform, NGOs and environmental organizations, an organizational structure is introduced, which is headed by well-known and famous local intellectuals who are appointed leaders, representatives and presidents of their groups.

An interesting point concerns the mobilization and the recruitment of new members. First, both movements consolidate their grip on the public sphere. The communities of practice are in no small part responsible for the value adding to the fields of religion and knowledge and through their strong appeal to the urban middle class, are taking over the public sphere.

In his paper on the emergence of a religious public, Salvatore (1998) argues that Islam as a public norm operates through strategies of staging virtue. Virtue is a model of legitimate behaviour:

> "Virtue is here conceived not, tautologically, as a moral endowment, a code of behaviour inherent in (however changeable) cultural assets or traditions, but as a set of competencies that cultural (and in our case religious) elites are called to craft, refashion and promote in order to impose and consolidate their grip on the public" (Salvatore 1998: 87).

Strategies of staging virtue are dependent on the rules of communication within a modern public sphere: Salvatore shows how communication of religious codes in the public sphere is used to induce so-called civilizing processes, that is, processes that shape the social habitus. In short, he is looking at the ways through which staging virtue becomes a formidable instrument for controlling people and pinpointing loyalties (Salvatore 1998: 117). Following the same line of argument, the middle class as an educational elite is able, not least through the construction of public spheres, to construct and promote models of civility.

The grip on the public, the civilizing processes, includes also disciplining and communicative technologies to impose patterns of control on the communities addressed, 'requiring more or less coherent packages of commitments, obligations and rights' (Salvatore 1998: 88).

Religion is a 'field' in communicative relationship with other 'fields'. In the emerging cultural politics, the 'field' of religion is the spearhead of new public spheres. In the line of Armando Salvatore's work, the Islamic (religious) public sphere is not an ideal normative type of reasoned communication, but is a stage where religiously grounded virtue is engendered through specific discursive and disciplining technologies.

Religion as a cultural tool in particular has the potential to appeal to the spiritual needs of the middle class and to legitimize public action of the communities of practice. Coming back to our ethnography of public spheres in Southern Thailand, religion plays a crucial role in delivering the blueprints for a new consensus among the middle class: contemporary urban Buddhist and Islamic movements attract significant numbers of that social stratum (Jackson 1989).

Let us take a closer look on religion 'going public'. More research needs to be done on the impact of religious renewal on public life:

> "Little attention has been paid to the way a reformed, puritan or pietistic appropriation of religion has itself influenced public religion" (Salvatore 1997: 53).

In our view the interrelationships of privateness and publicness have been obscured by the now fashionable concepts of 'civil society'. The question will be not whether and to what extent a civil society has developed, but rather, which public categories may fulfil the role to account for the tension between individualization and social cohesion.

At first glance, Songkla's people organization is a non-hierarchical space and a non-profit organization, in which all members are givers. Indeed, equality and the call for human rights and participation in decision-making is a key term in the movement's campaign. The core members are organizing themselves in a strategic group, are actively engaged in status building and form an educational 'elite'. Songkla Prachakom and the many groups and networks, friendship circles, environmental groups, conservation networks and discussion groups, that are intimately linked to the movement, build, in their own understanding, a moral core in a corrupt society.

The Songkla learning festival is directed towards the family and the children of Songkla, opening up new spaces, playgrounds, and learning activities to the children. The integration of children and the qualities of responsible parenthood, on education and the accumulation of knowledge principally underline the integrative role of being a responsible and competent parent.

The joyful and entertaining atmosphere of the activities and spectacles contributes to the huge attraction of the association and especially to the mobilization of new members. The communal spaces are also fun-spaces and spectacles, in which people enjoy themselves, have leisure time and come together in a picnic-like atmosphere. The traditional dress contributes to the carnival mood.

The moral regimentation of orthodox Islam contrasts with the joyful atmosphere of Songkla Prachakom's activities. The harsh eradication of fun-spaces seems to be an integral part of the Muslim campaign to clear spaces for Muslims in Patani. As Werbner (1996) has shown convincingly, the battles between mass popular culture with its music and carnivals and the pious lifestyle-apparatus of the orthodox are typical to the internal struggles of Islamic communities, between women and men, young and old men, and to the ownership competition in Muslim public arenas.

Public Religion: Religious Public Spheres Compared

Jackson argues that the most important developments in Thai Buddhism in terms of the political role of Buddhism are taking place outside the convention-bound hierarchy of administrative monks (Jackson 1989). Many members of the professional and middle classes have turned to a number of sympathetic monks to provide a religiopolitical justification for their aspirations. The increasing appeal of reformist monks is due to the changing relationship of the lay community and urban Buddhist movements. The middle class has been considerably disenchanted with the state-imposed Buddhist Sangha which is perceived to increasingly frustrate the spiritual needs and growing political aspirations of the urban middle class. Reformist monks develop an approach to Buddhist practice that demonstrates the value and relevance of Buddhism to contemporary lay life. Phra Bhudhadhasa Bhikku has been honoured as 'Thailand's greatest contemporary spiritual leader'.

The origin and growth of Buddhadasa's movement has been itself an influential model for the Buddhist-inspirited people's organizations of Bangkok, Songkla, Phetchaburi, Chiang Mai and Korat. Suchira notes that Bhudhadhasa and his younger brother, Dhammadasa, set up the *Dhammadana* Foundation to support activities such as *Suan Mokkh* (The Garden of Liberation), a library, a school, a press and the journal, *Buddhasasana*. *Suan Mokkh* became a spiritual centre of Buddhist ideology. Bhudhadhasa related to the outside world, was a prolific author of books, a lecturing monk in Thai universities and a spiritual guide with wide popularity and influence among social and intellectual circles in Bangkok. The nation-wide network and influence of Bhudhadhasa has been tapped by the provincial people's organizations, such as Songkla Prachakom.

Songkla Prachakom develops the Buddhist teachings of Phra Bhudhadhasa Bhikku into a powerful legitimizing force to defend liberal and democratic principles and campaigns. The teaching of famous monks on social problems, environmental awareness and Buddhist life conduct are recorded on tape and video and disseminated through private radio programmes, videotapes and during seminars and campaigns.

Bhudhadhasa maintains that Buddhism must be interpreted so that it is beneficial for modern people. His demythologized interpretation of *Nibbana* as being a spiritual condition attainable in this life appeals to the Buddhist lay consumers. As Jackson (1989) explains, the reformist monks, as epitomized by Bhudhadhasa, are intellectuals who approach Buddhism in terms of their rationalist view of Buddhist doctrine. This rationalist approach to the teaching leads the reformists to place considerable emphasis on morality and *Vipassana,* or insight meditation. Following the teaching of Bhudhadhasa, the middle class is aligning itself with a rational interpretation of Buddhist guidance of salvation, liberating the teaching from the traditional doxy and rituals. In the appropriation of religious forms, Buddhism is secularized, providing a cultural tool in serving the worldly ends of the movement.

Buddhist monks are invited to academic seminars and environmental campaigns, representing an authoritative language, following the tradition of lecture monks, which has been founded by Bhudhadhasa.

Buddhism is a crucial signifier of Thainess and Thai patriotism. The centrality of Buddhism in the discourse underlines the quest for authenticity. Buddhism has a central place in the definition of the locality, which is invented by the community (as home and place of birth). Buddhism is situated in the centre of community life, a pool of local knowledge, and a spiritual guidance in front of the ills of society. The emphasis on morality and rules cultivates differences between Buddhist and non-Buddhists. Buddhism underlines the Thai way of doing things and provides a religious meaning to secular political action.

Public Islam provides a powerful religious instrument in the hands of religious leaders to mobilize and discipline members. When the language of religion gains ground in public discourse, newer religious specialists acquire more power of definition of individual correctness and public morality. The rise of a modern public sphere and the development of a massive apparatus of lifestyles depends on the centrality of highly charismatic religious leaders, who are legitimized by their education in Saudi Arabia or Egypt. Those religious leaders, as epitomized by Ismail Lutfi are media-stars whose mediation of legitimate behaviour in public life is staged again and again in public speeches and in Islamic media. The media-stars are mass producers of Islamic media, such as pamphlets, books, and tapes.[1] The intellectual public sphere is based on the guidance and teaching of the religious authorities, who produce authoritized knowledge. The structural transformation of the Muslim public sphere entails an increasing autonomization of public players endowed with religious credentials, who 'make people talk' about what it means to be a good Muslim. Islamic publications address topics of immediate practical and emotional concern for most. The proliferation of the Islamic media indicates that religion operates in a field that is governed by the culture market (Raphael 1989). The staging of Islam as virtue is a game about enriching and stabilizing clienteles, as well as gaining power through maintaining audiences and followers (Salvatore 1998: 113). The religious discourse cultivates 'good Muslim' and 'bad Muslim' discourses, indicating a competition of high and popular religion. The high production of orthodox Islam hopes to domesticate and purify popular beliefs. This is done by intellectuals who increasingly go into the *pondoks* and villages to spread the messages of textual Islam. Moreover, Islamism cultivates dichotomizing Islam/ non-Islam and heaven/hell differences. The dynamics of distinction include stereotypes and rhetorical attacks against the Thai Buddhist. The mediation of the public sphere by the public heroes to the global Arab Islamic public sphere is very desirable for the articulate Malay-Muslim middle class. Furthermore, solidarities to the governing PAS in Northern Malaysia and friendships between charismatic religious leaders on both sides of the Thai-Malaysian border are established.

Women Merit Making (*tambun*), Kelantan, Malaysia.

Public Transcripts

It is argued that public transcripts of dominant groups still deserve more academic attention. The movements eagerly seek a presence in the public sphere. In Southern Thailand, the public sphere is emerging as a result of the tireless efforts of the urban middle class. This well-educated and articulate social stratum has an interest in disseminating its issues. The strategies of communication are not limited to games of representation to win over a public contest, but to construct and promote models of civility. Strategies of communication aim to control and discipline the members of the community addressed. In the process, the communities of practice aim to consolidate their grip on the public sphere. Thus, contrary to the hidden transcripts of the subaltern, the dominant groups are looking for visibility in the social arena. In the sense that the communities of practice are able to shift pattern of authority, they emerge as strategic groups (Evers/Schiel 1988). Strategic groups are able to impose their standards of legitimate behaviour on the social arena, and consolidate their position of power. The strategic groups in question produce and impose models of civility on the communities addressed. Religion is used as the spearhead of the discourses. Theoretically speaking, religion provides a powerful symbolic resource, enabling the community of practice to engage in forms of social representation. In the emerging monopolistic cultural markets, religious renewals are distinctive makers of the educated middle classes. Religion exemplifies the relationship of the private and the public in the communities of practice. The reformist, rational 'high' religious productions construct and promote models of life-conduct or models of inwardness. The field of religion is upgraded in the public sphere. Definitions of a 'good Buddhist' or a 'good Muslim' abound. In the process of shifting structures of authority and the transformation of the public sphere, the middle class segments aim to institutionalise their models of civilisation. As a result of the successful mobilisation and discipline of members, strategic groups emerge and transform a loosely structured core group into social institutions who are partaking and shaping contemporary public life in Southern Thailand. Thus, the 'Network for Political Reform' emerges as political force in Songkla, representing the new society and gradually gaining bargaining power in local politics. Their representatives proliferate as heroes of the public sphere who take a leadership role in community affairs and prepare themselves for positions in the local political system. As for orthodox Islam, the *pondoks* are semi-autonomous public spaces which indicate the dominant position of orthodox religious leaders in the Muslim public sphere. The ethnic Chinese reinforce their Chinese cultural identity in the public sphere as well.[2] Each cultural segment has been involved in a general pronunciation and essentialization of identity politics in the 1980s and 1990s.

The public spaces have been classified in Table 6, which aims to show the meaningful contents of communities in a comparative perspective:

Table 6. Cultural Public Spaces Compared

Commu-nities of practice	Perform-ance	Language	Religion	Media	Organiza-tion
Songkla Pracha-kom	*baan koet* campaign	Thai, southern Thai	Bhudhad-hasa	Core radio local media	Songkla Forum, NGOs, *wat*, politi-cal reform
Islamic intellec-tual cul-ture	Islamic sermon	Melayu, Arabic, Jawi	Islamic reasser-tion	Islamic media, tapes	Mosque, *pondok*, *Madrasah*
Chinese commu-nal life	Chinese rituals *Kwan Im*	Chinese, Thai	Chinese syncretism	Books, videos, television	Business associa-tion, tem-ple, alumni

As the communities seek visibility, local intellectuals are staging the urban event. The high visibility of seminars and campaigns, Islamic sermons and public speeches, and Chinese festivals express the cultural power of groups.

The somewhat essentializing identifications in the public sphere indicate the importance of the respective public spheres to provide the sites where new identities are constructed and where identities can be demonstrated within the demarcations of we-group formations. Language and religion provide the symbolic resources, underlining the ownership of the public sphere. The use of Thai, Malay, and Chinese languages and dialects (Southern Thai, Chinese dialects, local Bahasa Melayu) not only reflect language competencies, but contribute to the exclusive nature of the club, the Thai club being for Thai speakers and so on. The communities of practice construct and promote their localities, beliefs and media of communication.

The medium of communication in the prospectus, brochures and radio programme of Songkla Prachakom is central Thai. As for the neo-Islamist movement, the Melayu dialect is the main medium of communication. The use of the Arabic language enhances the religious credibility and prestige of the speaker and contributes in no small part to the profile of High Islam.

Significantly, as has been pointed out before, the communities of practice dispose of their own local media, being producers of media spheres. Core radio uses the central Thai language. Islamic media are available in Thai and Malay (imported from Bangkok or Malaysia). The *Islamic Guidance Post* is printed in Bangkok in the Thai language, as less and less people in the urban areas are able to read Jawi.

The models of civility are promoted through religious institutions, as epitomized by the mosque and the *wat*.

Modes of Social Organization and Leadership[3]

The two instances of cultural movements in Songkla and Pattani develop original modes of social and political organisation and social action that deserve to be dealt with in a special section.

Songkla Prachakom is composed of associations, friendship circles, NGOs, clubs and associations. In contemporary Songkla, a list of voluntary associations has been established and new groups also emerge. A sketch of some of these groups illustrates the character of Songkla's associations:

Songkla Forum is an organization that has been set up by Khun Pannipa and her husband and consists of people from the educational sector. Songkla Forum is a sister organization of Bangkok forum and an illustration of a new generation of NGOs. This NGO envisions to develop social creativity in the urban sectors of Thailand. Members join in seminars, workshops and training courses in order to study the history of places, temples, streets and quarters and to develop, animate and give vitality to urban communities. Songkla Forum aims to discover the roots of moral and spiritual leadership and autochthonous organization. Second, Songkla Forum aims to mobilize urban communities in order to challenge the urban administration. Thus, Songkla Forum combines a promotion of local knowledge, home and tradition with an appeal to participate in action and planning. Projects on social problems, such as children's education, the pollution in Songkla Lake or the conservation of the old city are systematically explored in seminars and workshops. Concrete demands and campaigns are prepared in training courses, which focus on team building and social creativity.

Songkla Forum provides a framework of learning. This purpose of learning is also reflected in the organizational framework as well. The core leaders of Songkla Forum consists of people from the educational sector in particular. These core leaders are perfectly located to give lectures to the people. They are doing so. Khun Pannipa Sotthibandhu and her husband act as moderators during seminars and workshops. During the Learning Festival, the highlight of Songkla Forum's campaign, key people from the educational sector taught about the social ills in Songkla, and of the possibility of overcoming these problems.

Pia for example has been involved in activities to protect slums from demolition in Bangkok. Pia and Leg explain that slums have developed in Nakhorn, Phuket, Trang and Songkla as a result of pressure in the rural areas to sustain a livelihood. More and more poor peasants in Southern Thailand are leaving the rural areas to find a place in the city. The city of Hatyai does not allow squatters to stay in the city at all. The NGO assists squatters to upgrade their housing, to build a hall for the slum community, to develop a community spirit, to build associations, and to represent the interests of the squatters in negotiation with the local government. Pia and Leg have completed a university education. They became interested in the problems of squatters during their participation in student clubs.

The NGO is member of a nation-wide network of voluntary associations working in urban areas and gets support from mother NGOs in Bangkok. The NGO in Songkla has a relative independence from the more experienced NGOs in Bangkok in terms of strategies and decision-making. The close cooperation with other organizations of Songkla Prachakom and a pragmatic attitude towards the authorities helped to put the problems of squatters on the agenda of the local state. The NGOs aim to slowly construct mutual trust and cooperation in the process of building reliable associations that could defend the interests of the squatters and enable them to negotiate with the authorities. Therefore, the NGO organizes hearings, that bring together representatives of the state, the NGO and the squatters.

The NGO enjoys financial support from international donor agencies, such as UNICEF and Miserior. The NGOs in Songkla consist of young volunteers who engage at the grassroots level, with squatters, small peasants and fishermen. The volunteers are led by more experienced people who are accepted as senior NGO leaders. The NGOs work in close co-operation with each other and increasingly co-ordinate their activities with the mother NGOs in Bangkok and the donor agencies.

The NGOs share some patterns of social organisation and leadership. Generally speaking, the emergence of some charismatic key people who become well-known personalities can be observed. In particular, the non-professional role of professionals and the role of professionals in social and political change deserve more attention (Evers 1974). In a situation of modernization, increasing specialisation and professionalisation in Southern Thailand, the non-professional role of professionals is increasing. Professionals such as doctors and representatives from the educational sector are highly regarded in society. In the politics of everyday life, they occupy respectable positions in urban society. Their enthusiastic participation in public life is recognized by the urban clientele who increasingly pressure for more important roles for their leaders. Furthermore, the professionals increasingly take up positions as consultants of dominant groups in the local state.

Not least due to the increasing importance of non-professional functions, some professionals become senior figures who are recognized as intellectuals and leaders. Thus, the status of these professionals is really upgraded in the public sphere. Professionals are regarded as a legitimate elite who base their credibility on their high education and their professional ethics. Associations also constitute the base of their status and reputation.

These public professionals draw on their new institutions in social and political life. In the process of building professional associations in Songkla, the role of these key figures also change. Professionals practise a full-time occupation (Evers 1974: 3), they are committed to rules of competence and enjoy substantial autonomy. In the local public sphere, these professionals become leading intellectuals who develop organizational bases of power and are increasingly successful in mobilizing, controlling and commanding segments from the urban middle classes in a junior position who feel attracted to the efforts and campaigns of leading professionals.

These professionals set the standards of morality owing to their educational specialization and pool of knowledge. The authority of these professionals is widely accepted and confirmed by all parties, including the local state, which increasingly depends on the competence of these leading professionals. As these professionals become strategic figures who design strategies and promote their norms and values in the public space, the local state increasingly attempts to incorporate them into state programmes.

The booming public life is not least due to the progress of democracy and decentralization in contemporary Thailand. In this context, the negotiation of the social order becomes more intense. The increasing authority of leading intellectuals sets the standard for an alternative worldview that argues for the inability of the local state to solve the problems and the competence of the public organizations to do so. This alternative worldview complains that the social and political system is characterized by 'moral decay', 'corruption', 'egoism', and 'ignorance' on the side of the bureaucracy. These problems are coupled with 'drugs', 'AIDs', 'family abuse', and so on. The new public organizations and the core group of leading intellectuals claim no less than the ownership of the public space. Interestingly, the worldview promoted by Songkla Prachakom couples private and public issues in one programme and vision, contributing to the strength of the message and the appeal to the newcomer.

Leading Professionals in Songkla, Religious Authorities in Patani

In the process of making their interests public and their worldview an authoritative language, the core group of leading professionals emerges as a central agent of social and political change. In a similar manner, Islamic authorities set the standards for a social and political programme.

As the non-professional role of professionals from the educational sector is increasing, journalists, doctors, lawyers and academics emerge as strategic figures. The leading professionals control a new resource: education and knowledge. Evers and Schiel indicate that a new resource is likely to produce strategic groups who aim to appropriate resources (Evers/Schiel 1988). Coming from the educational sector, leading professionals control the access to education and to positions within the educational field. In the process of modernization, the field of education is elevated. The educational profession is raised to a higher intellectual level.

The staff of the many educational institutions in Songkla co-ordinate more and more closely. By weaving face-to-face networks, the educational professionals gain relative independence from the state. Moreover, the fact that the mayor of Songkla has been a very respected teacher (*kru*) shows the popularity and ability of learned professions to fill positions of power and responsibility.

Academics from educational institutions enjoy high status and prestige in local society. As persons of education and knowledge, *ajaarns* are said to be particularly well-suited to take up leadership functions. The professionals are asked by the people to take up positions of responsibility for the general welfare of the community. The movement is considered a family, the professionals senior persons and their followers 'children'.[4]

The movement seems to have arrived at a critical stage: it has changed from a loose social circle of followers and friends to a potent, organized social force. In particular, the strength of the core group is greatly enhanced by the new constitution and the opportunities of political participation. The leaders of the core group have a realistic aspiration to being elected to state positions. The proliferation of strategies is a crucial shift in the organization and growth of the movement into a political force.

The Newcomer: Patterns of Mobilization and Disciplination

The mobilization of newcomers in large numbers enhances the representation of the urban middle class. Both public spheres in Songkla and Pattani reveal stabilizing patterns of social mobilization which aims to produce reliable members. From the perspective of the movement, the new member undergoes a period of socialization in which he/she changes from a passive idiot to a responsible, competent and knowledgeable citizen; he/she changes from a private person to a public person. The transformation of identity in the public sphere is a result of social training in which the new member is urged to adopt to a new, enlightened life praxis. The social training in both organizations concerns the re-organization of everyday life. The transformation of social identity happens in multiple, subsequent stages: the new member has to be mobilized for the purpose of the movement. Both instances emphasize the communitarian character of the movement, in which the new member quits ignorance for enlightenment.

This transformation of the person does occur on different stages. The new members of Songkla people and sister organisations are encouraged to participate in workshops and training sessions in order to develop a community spirit. The workshops and training sessions are organised and administered by the core group of leading educators. Participants are encouraged to overcome sentiments of egoism and material greed. In this line, the new members withdraw their individual interests for the sake of the community. The members submit themselves to the pedagogical authority of the core group.

The emergence of an Islamic public sphere involves religious speakers (communicators) and audiences. Purification of Muslim against non-Muslim styles determines social discourse. The interpretation of Islam to the ritual and strict rules of body behaviour is instrumental in the power politics and social practices of orthodox, intellectual leadership. The reconstruction of Islam in the religious public sphere provides the means to control and discipline the followers by staging Islam as public norm. Intellectual Islam as 'the transformation and internalization of the 'Sacred' establishes a framework in which the followers quasi-employ the techniques of the self on their way to becoming good and knowledgeable Muslims.

The dynamics of the Islamic public sphere operate within the transformation of life and society in Southern Thailand. The proliferation of religious players takes place within a framework of deep disturbance of self-esteem of Malay Muslim intellectuals. Consumers of religious discourses make contingent uses of the staged morals. Members are really empowered to change their lives in response to these stimuli. The performance of the intellectualisation of Islam in religious speeches greatly appeal to academics through whose brokerage the youth attend the mass meetings and internalise the discourses of the religious leaders. The religious leadership integrates them into the larger translocal community and, doing so, mediates between global religious forms and the local situation.

Thus, participation in the religious public sphere offers access to 'sacred' knowledge, education, and Islamic networks. The new members of the community undergo profound transformations in the Islamic public sphere. Religious players formulate the definitions of what it means to be a 'good Muslim'. The institutionalisation of the religious public sphere is made public and indeed 'visible' through the regimentation of rules and body styles in everyday life. Through appearances in dress, the new member shows the cultural competencies and the adoption of 'High' productions of cultural (here religious) authority.

The application of moral and habitual codes confines the realization of the Muslim self to Public Islam. The attendance figures for Friday mosque services or the number of women wearing *jihab* head covers, both of which are increasing at a remarkable rate, are indicators of the strict observance of Islamic rules. The transformation of the person under the guidance of Islamic teachers in Southern Thailand is remarkable. The sharp distinction between Muslim and non-Muslim styles is successfully communicated in the religious public sphere and results in the adoption of Arabic models that are emulated. The coercion into conservative body styles symbolizes and makes visible more general patterns of control and discipline. The key to patterns of mobilization and discipline are modern *dakwa* (mission) movements. Academics are put in high esteem in the Malay community and are among the most energetic reformers.

The institutionalization of the networks is an important process that deserves more careful attention. The transformation of networks into strategic groups points to the political agenda of respective locally-based social movements and to the political actions carried out by their members. The research indicates an extension of public spheres into the organization of everyday life.

Culture Building and the Politics of Expressive Identities

How accurate is it to speak of a resurgence of cultural politics and what are the causes of the shift to culture and identity in the contemporary world? In present cultural politics, ideology about gender, sexuality and home occupy the cultural codes of the state, the media and religious movements. The 1990s have seen a massive production of images about the Asian family. This points to a situation, in which the frontiers of the private and public are blurred and in which the supposedly private spheres are shifting, being reworked and redefined in the larger culture, religion, and polity. Seen from a framework of the politicization of the private, the reproduction of middle class cultural forms involves the creation of a domestic ideology and its permanent reworkings.

The social centrality of life orders and the dynamics of distinction resulting from the contests cannot be grasped in the context of the local context. The priority of questions of life methodologies and changing subjectivities has to be understood against a background of increasing world market integration and the establishment of new social fields in the making of a bourgeois society. It is argued that the middle class space is a space on its own and the space is shaped and defended through a constant elaboration of the borderline. Women and men are affluent consumers of cultural products or architects of identity. The new consumers are involved in a permanent competition and are eager to position themselves in the political, economic and cultural fields. We may be interested in the adoption of practices of young parents as well as in the processes by which an expanding class comes to define its own way of life and thoughts as civilisation or simply as human nature.

In the present cultural politics, ideologies of the family, gender and home and sexuality, masculinity and femininies occupy the cultural codes in social dramas of the state, the media, and social and religious movements. Cultural images of the "Asian family" and "Asian values" have been used by Asian political leaders for political ends (Pertierra 1999, Surin 1999). The making of a class boundary involves everyday work in the reproduction of cultural forms. Class is not an essentialist category. The production and consumption of culture is a process in which the spaces of class have to constantly be created. Class is constituted in relation to ethnic or gender categories. Thus, rather than being a fixed social reality, a we-group that is organized in a frame of class and identity is a construction that involves the maintenance of boundaries to the ethnic other.

The educated middle class makes use of cultural tools in an attempt to shape cultural spaces in an ongoing negotiation of identity politics. The social group of academics, professionals, teachers, lawyers, doctors and architects, entrepreneurs and civil servants makes its interest visible in space. The borderline, which was drawn with the poor and very rich is based on tertiary education. The expansion of the educational system has enabled a new generation of people to climb the social ladder. The threat of downward mobility, social instability and personal crisis makes the ideal of a modern lifestyle-apparatus desirable. The organization in socio-religious movements promises security in a state of personal uncertainty.

In Southern Thailand, a rapid social transformation is shattering the foundations of social life. The intervention of the state apparatus has increased the presence of state power in the local areas and the extension of state power is now penetrating nearly every sphere of daily life. While only a few Chinese families control the means of production, poverty in the rural sector is increasing. People 'know their place in society' (*ruujak tana kong tua eng*) as the old saying goes.

Life Orders in Southern Thailand

It is no accident that the construction of differences is organized along competitive life-orders. It is important to recognize that lifestyle acts are also orderings acts. In Southern Thailand, ethnic and religious systems vie for cultural superiority: the revivalist interpretations of religion are making great inroads.

Intellectual Islam and reformist Buddhism are both movements with global locations and milieus, which are channelled into the local. They are modern in the sense that they are based on education. The socio-religious movements and their discourses are attractive identity offers and demand adherence and loyalty at the same time. The religious systems are the cultural tools, which the communities of practice make use of. The contest for life-orders reflects the power constellations in Southern Thailand and the often frustrated desire to challenge them. Leaders demonstrate their moral superiority and, thereby, legitimize their moral leadership. This leadership in issues of morality and questions of life methodologies compensates for powerlessness in either political or economic domains. Practices of cultural distinction are practices of inclusion and exclusion. The young women and men whom I met are living in close proximity, and are neighbours, but maintain sharp boundaries and separate life worlds. It seems to me that the private sphere is politicized, overdone and exaggerated. Identity markers and ethnic emblems are made visible in the public space in practices of consumption.

Family Constructions and Gender Orders

The negotiation of the borderline is explored further. Practices of consumption and lifestyles, in addition to giving meaning to lives, also have a function of ordering social life. As Maila Stivens shows, anxieties about family constructs and gender relations seem to be a central feature of the principal cultural contests of Southeast Asia (Stivens 1998). From the base of the collapse of private/public dichotomies in the feminist literature, Stivens et al. conclude that an exploration of gender relations provides important ways to theorise the interplay between consumer culture, economy, polity and religious practice in the region. The nesting of the political action of everyday life in larger, ultimately global, structures of power is a challenging task. Contests around remade private spaces are predominant issues with frequent debate on proper and good families and proper and good lifestyles.

Family constructs and gender relations are negotiated on different levels of society. The Asian family discourse is a pivotal nexus between the global and the local. In the Asian family discourse, the wife/mother is considered the 'bulwark' against the social costs of modernity. State propaganda, media and religious movements have focused on the personal, highlighting the threats posed to the family and to women's 'traditional' roles. Thus, the family becomes a favoured site for expressing more general tensions and ambivalence about the costs of development. Stivens points out that the concern for women and gender relations is related to the entry of women into the labour markets. Women show a strong confidence in their abilities and are organizing themselves in women's networks and female spaces, giving voice and visibility to women in the public sphere. Sexuality is a key site in discourses of distinction. The discourse on sexuality is a main theme in the campaign for Islamic lifestyles. Muslims from Southern Thailand and neighbouring Malaysia regularly meet in discussion circles on law, morality, and questions of life organization. Veiling is a favoured site for expressing a critique of the sexual promiscuity of the Thai, the breaking up of families, infidelity and minor wives and symbolises the strong segregation of gender as a key element of Islamic culture. Dress is a strong marker of ethnic identity and difference as well as a marker of prestige. People associate messages with dress. In Southern Thailand, dress-styles are expressions of ethnic and religious affiliations. The codes of dress include visual modifications to the body, which set off affective processes that result in recognition by the viewer (Eicher 1995). Dress, in this sense, is a strong emblem of group identity or group solidarity. Islamic cloth underlines the ethnic and religious affiliation as well as the cultural competence of the wearer. Veiling in Thai institutions is a subject of ongoing debate. The Hijab crisis in 1987/88, in which female students were banned from studying for wearing their *hijab* in class, highlighted the negotiation of Muslim identity in a Thai nation-state in a dramatic way (Chaiwat 1994). The *hijab* crisis resulted in anti-Muslim practices and racialized accusation of Muslims as practicing un-Thai behaviour.

In the heightened conflict, Muslim students found six prayer mats, one ordinary mat, and one *telekong* (dress worn by Muslim women during their prayers) near the college doghouse. This insult showed the escalation of a conflict around Muslim dress as a powerful symbol of Muslim cultural identity. The *hijab* crisis showed the deficits of tolerance in Thai society and the pressure of assimilation. Yet, it also showed the subjective strategies of female students who want to express their religious education and growing self-confidence. In the College of Islamic Studies in Pattani, the *hijab* is almost obligatory and new students are urged to wear the *hijab*.

Religious systems and ideas provide the public platform for a shared morality. A puritan and highly regulated sexuality and segregation of gender adds to the general features of a highly modernist movement, which establishes a religious and social order and which jealously guards the rules. The family has become a favoured site of cultural competition. In the middle class world, the family is a treasure and a key to the symbolic forms of middle classness. The family needs to be nourished, developed and is a constant investment. Parents have understood that education has been the backbone of their social career.

The large investment of the parents in the education of their children is both functional and demonstrative. The large investment in schooling and the multiple schemes of private tutorials mirror the ambition and care, investment and time that the parents are willing to put into their children's development. The selection of schooling and tutorials in religion, language, traditional music and dance mirrors the reconceptualisation of parenthood and childhood within the nuclear family and is an eager attempt by the families to come as near as possible to an ideal family type, which is constantly reproduced in the media, in advertising, in glossy magazines and in television serials. This ideal family is elaborated in spatial texts, in housing, especially the mass-fabricated townhouse, and the townhouse in the townhouse cluster, which spatially demarcates the frontiers of the middle class. The dwellings in the new estates and the worries as regards to the schooling of children reflect not only the work that goes into the reproduction of cultural forms, or the couple's ability to pay to afford a certain lifestyle, but also reflect the eager need to protect the family, especially the children, from the ills of a decadent society, from social pollution, and from the negative influences of a 'bad' environment. The children are watched closely by their parents, the students are watched by their teachers and in general, gossip and rumors exercise social control on the lifestyles of the people. This over-protection of the family's heaven in important ways restricts the movement of people. People retreat behind the boundaries of their own family, and their own house, and the children grow up in safe places, kindergartens, schools, shopping malls, parks and gardens and temples. The retreat from an environment perceived as harmful is a characteristic typical to the new generation in urban environments. From a Goffmanesque perspective, society becomes a stage for the performance of actors, from where the segments and groups engage in everyday or spectacular performances of cultural codes and in which the codes are dramatized (Goffman 1959, 1974).

Conclusion

Debating Morality and the Nation in Southern Thailand

In the escalating cultural competition, standards of morality are stylized as questions of cultural distinction and political legitimization. During my fieldwork in Songkla and Patani in 1995/96 and in 1998, competitive life orders provided the cultural codes of a passionate discourse on good society. In the following, I want to show that the debate on morality reflects political struggles in Southern Thailand and that family constructs and gender relations are not only negotiations in the private sphere, but symbols which patrol the borders of the nation-state.

Wat Sathing Phra, Mural, Songkla, South Thailand.

After the Nation-State?

The nation-state has come under close scrutiny from scholars in Southeast Asia (Anderson 1983, Evers/Schiel 1988, Brown 1994). Generally speaking, the debate has benefited from a boom in post-colonial and post-modern studies which emphasize the fragmentation of political, economic, and cultural structures of the state in a context of transnationalism and globalization. Yet if we are honest, we know very little about how the nation-state is negotiated and contested in everyday life. This is, as Herzfeld (1997) notes, "because anthropologists have largely shunned the state or reproduced its essentialism by taking official ideology as the truth about what the nation-state is actually about." The notion of the state as a bounded entity is not helpful in understanding how people are influenced by the modern state. We propose to explore the ways in which people are negotiating the paradoxes and tensions between personal and national identity. The notion of the border is helpful in deconstructing the state and its mechanisms. In this framework, the border is not limited to the physical border, but includes borderlines on different levels, including ethnic and religious boundaries.

As Herzfeld (1997) explains, the anthropology of the nation should aim to avoid both top-down and -up approaches. We need to know how the various borderlines are negotiated in different cultural and social settings or arenas. Like Herzfeld, I make no excuse for comparing the cultural intimacy of morality to the intellectual baggage of what the nation is actually about. Nation-states like to describe themselves in intimate terms of home and kinship, which endorse the populations in their territories. The German Fatherland comes to mind, as does the intimate Thai terminology of 'home' (*baan*) and 'kinship' (*piinong*), including the members of the Thai family. Anderson's (1983) imagined community, which has been developed in the context of Southeast Asia, says very little about the reproduction and contestation of the nation in the symbolism, emotion and struggle of everyday life.

I recall a long interview with a civil servant in Yala, originally from the southern province of Phatthalung, whose wife is working for the government television channel 11. This bureaucrat always linked loyalty to issues of home and family. He added family-planning to a long list of what defines the good citizen and included Thai literacy, the performance of the Thai Wai greeting, and participation in Thai Buddhist rituals. He contends that Muslims think that family planning is against Islamic rules, that they have too many children, are not interested in education and that their children do not grow up as good citizens and compared this 'immoral' behavior with his own family situation and his perception that two children is an ideal family size to guarantee high education and good future prospects. The centrality of the family and its intimate link to the nation is not arbitrary or accidental. Rather, the family, the cultural images of the family, the discourse on the family and its organization and role are key discourses and symbol of the cultural contest in South Thailand and in the region.

In an informal discussion, a Muslim intellectual compared Thailand to a brothel and likened government officials to women and tea-money. Again, the family was brought up without my asking for it. Children are seen as a gift from God. Thai families who limit themselves to one or two children are ridiculed. Here too, family constructs and gender relations are in the centre of identity. Music and dance are seen as temptations to the body and should be forbidden. I remember a discussion in which a model student points out that the boys should cover their knees while playing soccer, because 'the Thai are watching us'. Sexuality is encouraged in the boundaries of the married couple and the private home. How often have Muslim teachers asked me about my private life and supposed that as a foreigner I will surely have a Thai girlfriend, although my partner and I were together, with our baby, during my fieldwork. The gossip and inquiry about the family is also an instrument of control.

Finally, the Thai Buddhist cosmopolitans in Songkla turn to the topic of Buddhism in order to describe what has gone wrong in the Thai 'home' (*baan koet*). Once more, the well-being of the family is singled out as a criterion for the well-being of society as a whole. It is said that in a time of change, greed and consumerism violate the social. Husbands stay away from home and drink alcohol. People do not respect the elderly and give up the local tradition. On the basis of home and family, my informants construct their visions, claims, and utopias for a good society. The representation of identity and modernity has a metaphorical, performative aspect, too. What is often dismissed as mere anecdote, are the stories that are crucial for the reproduction of national intimacy. As Herzfeld (ibid.) notes, by criticizing and complaining about the state, people also confirm and contribute to its shadowy existence.

Debating Morality

As Maila Stivens (1998) points out, in current debates on Asian values, the family and women's bodies loom large in the discourses of the states in Southeast Asia. In the current resurgence of identity and religion, family constructs and gender relations are being negotiated at the level of the individual and the level of the community. What is the rationality of debating and insistence on standards of moral behaviour? How about the purpose of cultural performance in public space? The communication of moral standards defines cultural identities and the boundaries of the social world. Moral behaviour is used to distinguish between good and bad, between us and them, in narratives of the self and of the other. It is the lifestyle, the food preferences, an item of dress, the organization of leisure, the participation in religious activities and meeting and avoidance practices that are used as boundaries of ethnic identity that can be displayed in public space. The discourse on the moral state of society should not be dismissed as anecdotal.[1] In Songkla and Patani, a resurgence of moralization has surely taken place.[2] The middle class takes on the roles of entrepreneurs and guardians of the mores. I have argued that the moralization creates both solidarity and contempt. The granting of moral qualities produces dignity and social recognition, whereas refusal to do so insults. Furthermore, I suggest that by using essential and binary oppositions of good and bad, social players (Buddhists and Muslims) negotiate power in the nation-state. It is by paying serious attention to subjective strategies of the self at all that we are able to decipher how people negotiate the nation-state and its political ideology in everyday life. By doing no more than looking carefully at different levels of social organization, we are able to "get inside this ongoing production of static truths" (Herzfeld 1997: 10).

The ideology of the state makes substantial use of metaphors of the body to define diligent moral behaviour (*khon dii*).[3] Stereotypes used in the ideological baggage contrast clean and dirty bodies. Bodies are regulated and disciplined in the Thai polity, especially in school. Negative stereotypes of the Malay Other include poor sanitation, fanatical bodies, veiled bodies or racial remarks. Development focuses on the regulation and control of the body in the streets. Practices of reformist Buddhists in Songkla and resurgent Muslims in Patani focus centrally on the control and the discipline of the body, strategies of embodiment and enselfment. Reformist Buddhists emphasize the relationship between body, mind, and society. The loss of social stability and comfort in the contemporary urban environment of endless disruption and homelessness characterizes the pathological body: greed and stress are the results. The body is harnessed by contemplation and meditation. Radical Muslims in Patani apply Shari'a laws in the regulation of bodies. Thus, ironically, teachers, politicians and intellectuals use official idioms in the pursuit of highly unofficial personal goals (Herzfeld 1997: 2-3). The social players, Thai Buddhists and Malay Muslims, use cultural forms in direct opposition to the state. The everyday rhetoric of Thai Buddhists in Songkla and Malay Muslims in Patani are different parts of the same communicative system centring on the protection of the body from the harmful influences from the West (Horstmann/ Schlee 2001). Ironically again, the embodiment of the moral discourse of social actors in Songkla and Patani participates in the reproduction and stabilization of the political ideology of the nation-state by playing according to the state's rules.

Political Careers in Songkla

Using terms related to home, belonging, and place of birth, civil groups aim to build up emotional bonds to Songkla. Borrowing from the discourses of Thai intellectuals, the concept of community culture (*watthanatham chumchon*) is praised in an attempt to discover local identity and to establish what 'the local' is in relation to Bangkok. The communal framework makes use of the spiritual resources of the Bhudhadhasa movement, which has followers in all parts of Thailand in academic and intellectual circles (Suchira 1991). The movement has been led and institutionalized by a core group of local intellectuals who have taken a grip on Songkla's public space. These core people are senior figures from educational institutions, such as the Ratchapat Institute, the Teacher's College, Thaksin University and Prince of Songkla University. The team is supported by a number of groups and networks such as NGOs, environmental groups, individual professionals, community media, and Buddhist foundations.

The Bhudhadhasa movement adds moral weight and spiritual meaning to the production of locality. The emphasis on human development serves to keep it distinct from both the world of economic profit and political power. The organization quickly incorporates representatives from the business world and the local government of Songkla. Conversely, civil society is quickly absorbed by the state. Local leaders are not turning against the state; indeed, they have political ambitions themselves and strive for individual careers in the parliamentary system.

The leadership uses the community media as a springboard to develop their personal political style, to become prolific a media star, and to propagate political strategies. While the leaders stress their proximity to political power, the lack of political power is of concern to the project for political reform and democracy in particular. The leadership admits the lack of executive political power in their report summarizing the activities of the groups (see Vichai 1998).

While the people's organizations arrange numerous seminars to promote the fruits of political reform, they hardly seem able to apply the new laws at all. Thus, rather than challenging the state, some leaders prepare the ground for their own personal careers in formal political processes. In contrast, the focus on the field of life politics is partly a result of the political limitations of local groups. The people's organizations set the rules for an expansion of public spheres, in which new fields, family, the quality of life, nature, and Buddhism are occupied by Songkla's rising middle class groups. While hitherto the financial support for NGOs came from international donor agencies and continues do so, Songkla Prachakom enjoys the financial support of the local government and local business. This endorsement illustrates the new role of Prachakom in promoting social integration. However, it also highlights the dilemma of being incorporated into the strategies of business and state.[4] The groups aim to change the political system from 'within,' but–as the leaders themselves admit–they largely fail to do so.

The cultural tools of Songkla Prachakom are significant building elements in negotiating Thai culture. The revitalization of local traditions and crafts points to a process of local self-consciousness and self-assertion. Songkla's people's organizations are in active contact with other middle class groups in Thailand, such as *klum rao rak* Phetchaburi, Bangkok Forum, or groups in Nakhorn Sri Thammarat. The image of the Thai family is upheld, but the Southern Thai roots are emphasized. The organizations are integrated into Buddhism, but appropriate the modern, intellectual discourse of Phra Bhudhadhasa to legitimize their intervention in public life. The people's organizations constitute a patriotic movement that stresses the independence of Songkla in relation to Bangkok, but that nevertheless calls Southern Thailand 'home.' Thus, Thainess is reproduced at the boundaries of the movement.

In the long run, Songkla Prachakom may develop into a more formalized, more rational association that stabilizes the local state and provides it with much needed legitimacy to rule. The key figures in the core group are already preparing themselves for big political careers. The core group will have to deal with the integration of competing sets of parties and discourses, such as the Hatyai Chamber of Commerce, the slum communities of Songkla, the peasant communities around

Songkla Lake and the NGOs. *Ajaarn* Aree Rangsiyogit explains to me
that the parties have had to adjust to the purpose of Songkla Prachakom. Thus, The leadership has to fulfil the Herculean task of mediating
between conflicting interests. The leadership borrows from discourses
of Thai intellectuals, such as Dr. Prawes Wasi.

The transformation of the Thai locality in Songkla is deeply embedded in the cultural transformation of Thailand. Discourses on local
wisdom and community culture are flourishing in academic and intellectual circles (Suchart 1999a, 1999b), and the master discourse of Mor
Prawes Wasi is a very influential discourse in contemporary Thailand.

Leading Thai intellectuals are invited in to legitimize the people's
organizations. Mor Prawes Wasi was invited to open the provincial
Songkla Prachakom in 1996, in which the local Thai state, people's organizations, and NGO's are supposed to co-operate. Likewise, the respected politician and businessman Anand Panyarachun was invited in
1997 to legitimize the Political Reform project which would implement
the new constitution in the face of resistance from the old establishment in Songkla/Hatyai.

The social network of the Songkla Thai middle class integrates ideas in a process of increasing national integration, while the strong emotional construction of locality pushes a form of Thai-Thai identity. The
people's organizations in Songkla are well embedded into a national
network of 'people's organizations' called city-net. This network comprises the urban middle class and focuses on lifestyles.

New developments in Buddhism play a conspicuous role in sup-
porting the legitimization of Songkla Prachakom. The people's organizations in Bangkok, Chiang Mai and Songkla use reform Buddhism as
an instrument of power. The reception of rational, scientific interpretations of Theravada Buddhism is used to legitimize visions, claims and
utopias of a just moral order and the political participation of the urban
middle classes. The teachings of reformist monks (Phra Bhudhadhasa,
Phra Thepwethi, Phra Paisan and Phra Panyanantha) are cited (see
Jackson 1989).

The core group of a dozen or so people in Songkla Prachakom have
become very powerful figures in Southern Thailand. The movement
derives from the closely knit social network of these few core members. They are preparing for political careers in political parties, in local
government, as senators, members of parliament. In the future, the
network may well transform itself into a formal institution, such as the
'political reform project.' Public Buddhism is used as a cultural tool and
spiritual umbrella to legitimize the activities of Songkla Prachakom and

for secular ends. The ideas are derived from contemporary Thai intellectual discourses on 'local wisdom' which engage the Thai state in a
debate about development. Thus, discourses on 'local wisdom' and
'Buddhist spirituality' are not local discourses, but are part of national
and global NGO discourses on alternative development. A relatively
unorthodox interpretation of Theravada Buddhism is used for secular,
political ends. The reinterpretation of Thainess and citizenship in the
boundaries of Songkla Prachakom is central to the efforts of core
members to push for a local identity which on the one hand permits
the strengthening and demarcating of the locality and on the other
hand is aloof enough to help support the ambitions of southern Thai
personalities to participate in politics on a national level. In summary,
the people's organizations in Songkla are attempting to organize civil
society in Songkla/Hatyai on their own.

Thus, People's organizations" develop in conjunction with the rise
of regional identity and new urban self-confidence. The transformation of the Songkla locality is developing in tandem with new developments in reformist Buddhism and its critics in contemporary Thailand.
The construction of 'Buddhist spirituality' derives from discourses of
popular Thai intellectuals on the Bangkok scene. The people's organizations, which are dominated by a handful of influential persons, succeed in mediating between competing political interests, business,
NGOs, and labor, promoting social integration under the umbrella of
Songkla Prachakom. The foundation 'Love Our Hometown' (*rak baan
koet*) helps sustain a local identity. Similar foundations have been established in other towns in Thailand, e.g. in Phetchaburi and Patthalung.

The people's organizations are organizing civil society in close relation to the local Thai state. In doing so, local Thai agency is negotiating
the relationship between centre and periphery in contemporary Thailand. In fact, Songkla Prachakom's core group has domesticated the
NGOs, changing their anti-state attitude, and involving them in co-operation and interaction with the local government. In this way, the people's organizations have participated in the re-constitution and
functioning of the local state and its policies; for instance, the mayor of
Songkla has given an address to the media in which he explains that the
local government needs the assistance of people's organizations to
cope with 'pressing problems'.[5]

Local activities are subtle forms of local appropriation of the state
that tend to stabilize its structures and provide it with additional legitimacy. Thus, the local state endorses and supports the activities of
Songkla Prachakom. As a result, locality and local state constitute each

other mutually. The nature of the state and the nature of the people's organizations are transformed as a result of this interaction. The social integration of civil society under the umbrella of locality help stabilize the local state, while the national networks of Songkla Prachakom in turn help stimulate and reinforce the process of national integration. Meanwhile, academic and professional leaders of the locally-based social movement have emerged as a strategic group that is increasingly able to spread its discourse through organizational structures and community media. Indeed, the inclusion of Songkla Prachakom in the political process may result in a hybridization and inclusion of individual members in the state (Evers/Schiel 1988).

Cultural Bonds Between Patani and the Middle East

Focusing on the negotiation of Muslim intellectual figures, positions, and locations in the changing Muslim public sphere, I show how local stages of Muslim social virtue are embedded within systems of reference to the Middle East (Horstmann 1999). Muslim intellectuals reconstruct the centrality of the Patani locality for the early spread of Islam in the Malay Peninsula in the fifteenth century. Hurgronje notes (1931) that the Patani *ulema* in Mecca established close links with their communities back home via religious students who came on pilgrimages. The emergence of transnational social spaces in the latter part of the nineteenth century created the bonds of Patani to the Middle East and contributed in no minor way to the influence of Islamic reformist thinking in Patani. The protracted conflict of the separatist Malay movement drew the attention of the Muslim world and strengthened connections to the Islamic heartland. One result has been an unprecedented flow of external resources for Islamic education. Traditional institutions of Islamic knowledge have been challenged by recent attempts of Muslim scholars at purifying them and at introducing the sanctity of 'authentic' Islam. In the local cultural transformation and process of Islamic self-awareness, Islamic locality and local knowledge is being reconstructed by way of language, methods of breathing and reading, of imagining, of dressing, and approaching the social 'other' (Stauth/Buchholt 1999, Introduction). The restructuring of Islamic education, the introduction of new dress codes, the reordering of gender relationships intensified in the latter 1990s as new ideas and worldviews were introduced by Middle East-educated urban scholars. The traditional imams of the Sufi tradition are losing their grip on Islamic public space. They are being replaced by Shari'a-oriented religious specialists. The restructuring of the Islamic school by orthodox scholars has profound implications for the way local Islam and Islamic lifestyles are reproduced in Patani Muslim society. The streamlined *pondoks* provide the basis for the social reputation and social power of scholars such as Dr. Ismail Lutfi. His free communication with Middle-Easterners, his having lived and studied in the Middle East and his knowledge of Arabic give Lutfi prestige in academic and intellectual circles. His staging of Islam as social virtue and public event in Patani, Yala, and Narathiwat is a new way of communicating Muslim authority in the Islamic public space. The authentic Islam is a convincing cultural tool for the cultural autonomy and social organization of the Malays in Patani. Lutfi and his followers aim to reorganize the traditional system of Islamic education and to streamline it according to purist and scripturalist lines. The increases in Mosque attendances, Islamic attire, Halal consumerism, and staging of Islamic virtue are related to cultural globalization. The reconstruction of local Islam in Patani is linked to the Islamic resurgence in Malaysia. The reformist Islamic mass movement provides a seductive role model and option for identification. The revitalization of the Malay language and Malay culture among academic and intellectual circles in Malaysia is a source of identification for Patani Muslims. Cross-border movements are increasing in importance and facilitate Muslim networks between Patani Muslims and Islamic movements in Malaysia. Muslim scholars from Southern Thailand are in touch with the *ulema* which represent the leadership of the Islamic Party, the PAS, which governs in Kelantan and Trengganu. Apart from informal Malaysian-Patani Muslim circles and study groups, Patani Muslims benefit from opportunities in higher education, in Islamic studies. Being Muslim, speakers of Malay, and Thai citizens, Patani Muslims develop multiple forms of political and cultural citizenship. The presence of the Islamic media, the impact of Islamic images from the Muslim world and the rise of the *Hajj*, the pilgrimage, have strengthened the connections of Patani, which hitherto has been so marginal to the Muslim world, to the Islamic heartland. The global character of locality does not impede Muslims' participation in the national political process. The Patani Muslim community is represented in the Thai parliament and seeks to achieve cultural autonomy through participation on the Thai political stage. The increasing presence of the Thai state, education, language, and Thai media in Patani does not lessen the identification with the *umma*. The re-construction of Islam under the leadership of scholars is a political strategy, the aim of which is to negotiate autonomy for Muslims in Patani.

Transformation of Locality in Southern Thailand: Visions, Claims and Utopias

It is interesting to compare locally-based movements in Songkla with Bhudhadhasa's reformist Buddhist movement. Bhudhadhasa's movement has been carefully analysed by Suchira (Suchira 1991): it began with a core of only four or five local people in Chaya who gathered to discuss religious problems. His ideas, disseminated through his many writings, provided the basis for an urban religious movement. Suchira argues that the expansion of Bhudhadasa's movement derives from Bhudhadhasa's teachings. His sermons and lectures were tape-recorded and published by his followers. A striking feature of Buddhadhasa's movement is its organization. So informal is its organization that many of its followers were led to believe that it has no organization:

> "There are neither criteria nor a set of tests for distinguishing those who are accepted for membership from those who are not; no committees and official duties of any kind; no law and rules within the movement; no regular pledges of financial support were organised" (Suchira 1991: 256).

Bhudhadhasa's movement is a fluid-type of organization in which many special-purpose sub-groups form and disband. Followers have organized themselves to spread the teaching through activities such as the establishment of forest monastic centres, public libraries, press houses and face-to-face talks. Bhudhadhasa's movement spreads unofficially, through various forms of communication, including word of mouth. Although the movement has no formal members, it is characterized by intimacy and devotion.

Special sub-groups form and disband within this fluid-type of organization. No census of followers is ever taken, and there are no institutional devices for recruiting followers. This very fluid-type of organization has not come about because of an inability to set up an effective organization. The flexibility of the movement seems to be its strength and contributes in no small way to its rapid spread and expansion. Followers identify themselves as members on the basis of their personal religious understanding and not the basis of formal membership. Some scholars refer to the followers of Bhudhadasa as 'unorganized masses'. Bhudhadhasa's movement took no step towards challenging any of the established Sangha with an organization of its own. Life and teaching at *Suan Mokkh* (the garden of liberation) has a special meaning. *Suan Mokkh* does not function as an administrative headquarters with branch offices but as a "centre of ideology" (Suchira 1991: 257). It can be said that *Suan Mokkh* has become the most influential spiritual center of reformist Buddhism in academic and intellectual circles in contemporary Thailand. The monk-followers of Bhudhadhasa have become very influential public intellectuals.

As to the structure of Songkla Prachakom, a closely-knit network of professionals, university lecturers, teachers, doctors, lawyers, judges, and entrepreneurs organizes itself in committees and its members occupy positions such as president, vice-president, etc. It would seem that there are no formal members and no sanctions against members. The motivation to join the movement seems to derive from the social recognition obtained by participation in the activities of the people's organizations. The rise of the movement is connected with the process of urbanization and urban culture. Volunteering and sharing are not only a ways of growing, but also a means of discipline or even an instrument of social control.

'Bhudhadhasa changed my life', is a phrase often repeated by respondents. Both monks and lay followers change their life conduct as a result of their involvement with the movement. The cultural construction of livelihood or lifestyles is a crucial dimension of participation in and personal devotion to the movement. The life-conducts, the new manner of breathing, meditation, attire and the food, adopted in the movement are new skills and habitual forms that are developed to find solutions to individual crises. Thus, Locally-based movements are intensively involved in the cultural re-construction of family and gender relations, in which the reception and processing of globalized images of family, love, and sexuality play such an important role. 'Chinese' cults and ritual practices in the south, 'Thai-Buddhist' reformist ideas and morals and the Islamist re-construction act as innovative agents in the making of moralities in contemporary Southern Thailand. The incorporation of *Kuan Im* into Thai society as an icon has arisen from her securely based presence in multiple sacred sites and spaces in the south (Hamilton 1999). The rapid spread of her influence into Bangkok and throughout the country has resulted from her identification with forces and lifestyle that are associated with virtue, renunciation, celibacy, and compassion. The most important aspect of her presence is the quelling of negative spiritual forces through the operations of her own compassion. *Kuan Im* is also central to the upsurge (or establishment) of those meditation, worship, and chanting groups popular particularly with women, which is a continuation of popular religious practice. Her elevation to cult status among the urban Thai Buddhists brings back into view elements of cultural practice and identity that had been consciously or unconsciously suppressed.[6]

The formula of the Thai intellectual Prawes Wasi, 'local wisdom,' is taken up to counter that which is seen as a shaking of the foundations of Thai Buddhist culture. Playing out the role of the 'parent,' it is not an accident that particular attention is given to the Thai youth and to the Thai children. In the beginning, the social movement tackled social problems such as pollution, AIDS, and drug abuse. Civil groups used reformist Buddhist philosophy to legitimize their activities. Later, political reforms raised considerable hopes for the political participation of the movement's informal leadership. Muslims also have to respond to the Thai public sphere as a stage where Muslim identity and culture have to be performed. So we can only speak here of an Islamic public culture as an appendix to the Thai public culture. This becomes even more obvious if one relates it to the sphere of public education and the different ways in which Islamic education is related to this. It is important to understand that the construction of the family, gender relations, women's place, and women's dress are important sites of the local cultural reconstruction of Islam, in which local conceptualizations are embedded into systems of reference to the Middle East and in which Arab symbols are channeled into local Muslim *pondoks*. The recreated construction of family, gender, love, and sexuality maintains the moral boundary to the Thai Buddhists and constitutes an explicit criticism of sexual practices in Thai urban culture. In addition, the institutionalization of gender seclusion and veiling in the Islamic school in a minority situation is a break with Thai Buddhist 'normality,' in which the *Hijab* is a symbol of otherness (Chaiwat 1994).[7]

Locality, the Public Sphere and the Making of Moral Space

The visions of the people's organizations in Songkla are derived from reformist-Buddhist social movements, networks, and ideas, which spread rapidly in Thailand. Bhudhadhasa's movement in particular has inspired popular Thai intellectuals and has expanded quickly to the national and even global level. The idea of a 'good life' is rapidly expanding to other places in urban Thailand, such as Korat, Chiangmai, and Phetchaburi. The teaching is directed at the laity rather at monks. Buddhism is interpreted as a way of life. As Ajarn Aree Rangsiyogit says:

"Buddhism has become fossilized. We desire a Buddhism engaging in this worldly activity."

Suan Mokkh, the forest hermitage, reflects Bhudhadhasa's revitalization of the forest monk tradition as well as his ideals to promote the substance of Buddhism. The monks lead their lives simply and close to nature. The focus is a modern building, which is called the 'spiritual theater' and which is used as an audio-visual center where Buddhism is propagated through paintings, slides, and films.[8] As Pannipa explains:

> "We want to use Buddhadasa's Buddhism as a spiritual umbrella for our activities."

The production of locality is expanding to the global level, spreading Bhudhadhasa's ideology from *Suan Mokkh* to Songkla, Bangkok and to the United States.[9] The expansion of Bhudhadhasa's movement was facilitated by his monk followers (such as Phra Pannananda in Nonthaburi, Bangkok), who spread Bhudhadhasa's teaching. A Buddhist organization on the lines of *Suan Mokkh* has been established in Chiang Mai. A Native American monk follower, Phra Santikaro, is disseminating Bhudhadhasa's writings in English and travels widely in Asia and the United States. He is serving as acting abbot of the new training community of foreign monks at *Suan Mokkh*.

The transformation of Islamic locality is occurring in the frame of the south-south patterns of cultural exchange and religious diffusion. Islamization in relation to Middle-Eastern systems of reference in marginal spaces such as Patani attracted unprecedented external assistance and attention from the Muslim world, especially from Saudi Arabia. This breed of new scholars is acquiring a specific habitus, which is a hybridization of local and Arab styles and languages. Scholars make ample use of Western technologies and media to propagate the new teaching. The ideas of Lutfi and his guru-followers can be described as utopian thinking (Maaruf 1999):

'In utopian thinking, the collective unconscious, guided by wishful representation and the will to action, hides certain aspects of reality. It turns its back on everything which would shake its belief or paralyse its desire to change things.'[10]

In the utopian mentality, Lutfi aims to imitate the sanctity of Medina in Thailand. The Islamic networks of Lutfi and his followers extend to Bangkok, Kelantan, Malaysia, Egypt and Saudi Arabia.

Debating Morality in Southern Thailand

Nostalgia is a driving force in a discourse on the moral crisis. Revealingly, communities in Songkla and Patani all participate in nostalgia and homesickness. Thai Buddhist and Malay Muslim segments of the new middle class find advantages in using cultural images of the past in their attempt to shape cultural space. Government officials and healers from Kuala Lumpur and Malacca are looking for the original cradle of Islamic education in Patani, participating in Friday prayers and discussion groups on Islamic morality. They are looking for the sources to authenticate their religious experience. They look at rural Patani as a cradle of Islamic civilization that converted early to Islam. The urban is devalued as a site of consumerism and desire, and the marginal is being upgraded as authentic and pure. In Songkla, teachers and artisans collect old photos of the past Songkla. Here again, the city is devalued as anonymous and cold. The old local culture is described as warm and lively. The temple, it is said, was once the center of the community, neighbors used to help each other, and the young would respect the old. In trips to Siam villages in Kelantan and Kedah, they are attracted by the minority status of famous abbots or want to visit villages on putative pilgrimage routes. Revealingly, nostalgia is also a key part of the ideological baggage of the nation-state, which constantly repeats the grandeur of the past, the goldenness of Thai civilization and the legitimization of the royal family as a parent of the Thai nation. Herzfeld (1997) argues that,

> " ... ironically, by reformulating or outflanking the official idioms, politicians, teachers, and intellectuals of different color participate in the validation of the state as the central legitimizing authority over their lives. By complaining about the moral crisis, in an ethnic style, or simply by talking of 'it' *they all contribute to making the state a permanent fixture in their lives*" (Herzfeld 1997, emphasis added A.H.).

In this sense, transnational Thai Buddhists who invent pilgrimage routes in northern Malaysia and transnational Muslims who consume sermons of Malaysian shaikhs on the Islamic organization of the family and gender are more integrated into the Thai nation than ever. The identity politics in Southern Thailand construct and shape the communal space in local and global forms of communication. Lives in South Thailand are presented and negotiated in the cultural space of national intimacy. The idea of morality emerges as a central, yet conspiciously neglected category of the intellectual contest, which is played out in South Thailand in the nineteen-nineties and beyond. In the escalating cultural competition, identities of moral communities are essentialised, but have a common focus: the intimacy of morality.

Notes

Notes to Introduction

1 The framework of the expanded public sphere has been provided by Habermas (1979). See Calhoun (1992) for a discussion of the public sphere in different historical contexts.
2 Many Thai scholars examine the question of why Malay speaking Muslims do not assimilate into Thai society (see Chaiwat 1992). Here, the prejoritive construction of Malay Muslim identity is used as a starting point of research. One imagines that the cooperation of Muslims is not very great.
3 The empirical study of borderlands and border identities is a fascinating field which has just begun to appear in Southeast Asia. See Donnan/Wilson (1999).
4 For a theoretical concept on cultural boundaries in the context of multi-cultural society and political arena, see Schlee/Werner (1996) and Horstmann/Schlee (2001).
5 For studies on Indonesia with a similar outlook, see Galizia (1996) and Prodolliet (1996).
6 The political role of the middle class in Thailand and in Southeast Asia has been after a hesitant start marked by an explosion of interest on the subject at hand (Embong 2001, Sungsidh/Pasuk (1993), Tanter/Young 1990, Ockey 1992/1999, Rüland 1999).
7 As Lee/Ackerman (1997:10) note, 'the opening up of religious markets on a global scale has been possible because of the rapidity of travel and the worldwide linkages of communication, but more signicantly these developments have been accompanied by an increasing process of individualization in which the quest for religious meaning is becoming more and more a personal affair.'

Notes to Chapter 1

1 See Ackerman/Lee (1988) for a detailed account of 'Migrants, Merchants, and Missionaries on the Golden Peninsula', pp. 10-33.

2   Hurgronje (1931) reports that the Patani *ulema* in Mecca established strong links with their communities back home via religious students who came on pilgrimages to study with them.

3   For a full translation, see the appendix in *The Story of Lady White Blood* in Gesick's wonderful study (1995: 84-86).

4   The importance of the Chao Mae Lim Ko Niew public event was addressed at the official opening ceremony by the deputy prime minister of the central government who addressed a Chinese dragon, asking: 'Do you speak Thai?' Opening his speech by saying: 'My fellow countrymen, brothers and sisters,' he remarked on the alignment of the Thai nation-state with Chinese business groups. In addition, he gave a stear warning to the Muslims and warned that the Thai government will not tolrate Islamic radicalism (author's own observations).

5   Television and radio are required by law to provide certain programmes that strengthen national identity and national unity. Audiences are required to stand still, leave off whatever they are doing, and respectfully observe the period during which the anthem is broadcast, while carefully chosen images of the King and country appear on the screen. These images comprise situations in which members of the royal family are shown among the 'plain folk', underscoring the epithets of a benevolent father and stressing his care and responsibility for the people. Through the influential medium of television, the monarch is staged in even the remotest parts of the country, including the hill tribes of the upper North and the Muslims of the Lower South. Just as the King and the royal family came to symbolize the nation, the monarchy has provided a means to overcome the ethnic divisions in Thai society and to integrate the minorities in the organic body of the nation (Hamilton 1991).

6   I am grateful to Michele Lamont whose study: *Money, Morals and Manners* has inspired the drawing of a portrait of middle class men. With a similar focus on cultural distinction, Lamont explores the subtle cultural boundaries of upper-middle class men in France and the United States (Lamont 1992).

7   The distinction of locals and cosmopolitans is developed by Hannerz in order to describe the positioning of people in world society (Hannerz 1992, 1996).

Notes to Chapter 2

1   See the introduction in: Sen/Stivens (1998).

2   As Purushotam writes, 'to be middle class is to do the work of making the relevant choices from within this vast arena. It is not just a
matter of making choices per se; the choices must add up to a complex whole. This is because, third, choices must be balanced by a realistic appraisal of what is possible. This is underscored by the
notion that the wrong choices can cause the loss of upward momentum, the stuff of middle classness' (Purushotam 1998: 129).
3   The illustrative vignettes of some families show that the women
have been the more outspoken, much more articulate partners and
that they have been much more reflexive about the processes of
constructing a family.

Notes to Chapter 3

1   For a more detailed interpretation of the movement in a comparative perspective, see Chapter 5 on cultural politics.
2   See the brochure of *Songkla Forum*, No. 4, September/October
1997 for more details on the children's excursion and the painting.
3   The discourse on reviving local Thai communities and Thai values
is to be found in the position of *Khun Pannipa Sotthibandhu* (see be-
low) of Songkla Forum and in the accompanying print media.
Communitarian values can be seen as being a crucial component in
constructing the essential cultural identity of contemporary Thai
intellectuals (Suchart 1999, Surin1999).
4   A return to national Thai values and a culture based on family, kinship, and community is advocated by communitarian intellectuals.
Among the most prominent are Chai-Anan (1997), Chatthip (1994)
and Prawes Wasi (1999).
5   See Chapter 4 on community media for an elaboration of the importance of locally-produced media.
6   Anand Panyarachun was held in high regard and seen as representing all the important Thai values for his reform-mindedness, anti-
bureaucratic orientation, incorruptibility and honesty. He played an
important role in the constitutional reform of 1995, 1997. He per-
sonifies the values for a modernising and globalising society (Surin
1999).
7   See Chapter 4 on the media as a springboard for political careers
and the Concluding Remarks for an outlook on vision and political
inclusion.
8   The weakness of the movement to challenge traditional society has
been referred to in the report by Vichai Kanchanasuwon (Vichai
1999).

9   In the following section, 'Patani' is used with one "t" to name the
    Islamic locality as a whole, whereas 'Pattani' with two "tt" I used to
    designate the small town of Pattani in *Changwat* Pattani.

10 In the following section, 'Malay' is used to name the Malays in
    Thailand. The great majority of the Malays are Muslims.

11 The history of Patani is a sensitive issue which is rarely addressed
    by the Thai government. The Tourist authority of Thailand pro-
    motes the 'Deep South' as a region 'where Thai Buddhists and
    Thai Muslims harmoniously co-exist.'

12 This middle-class segment achieved its new status through tertiary
    education. I argue that this segment of local intellectuals is critical
    in forming and transforming the Islamic public space and in set-
    ting the standards.

13 This special relationship is described in Roff's reader on Kelantan:
    Religion, Society and Politics in a Malay state (Roff 1974). in par-
    ticular, see the Chapter by Haji Salleh on the life and influence of
    guru To Kenali, the Chapter by Roff on the Kelantan *ulema* and the
    Chapter by Kessler (1978) on Muslim identity and political behav-
    iour.

14 In the previous Thai government led by the Democrats, the For-
    eign Minister was Dr Surin Pitsuwan, a prominent Muslim mem-
    ber of the Democrat party and author of *Islam and Malay
    Nationalism* (Pitsuwan, 1985).

15 In accordance with Geertz (1968), the new religious style is called
    'scriptural Islam' here.

16 The reintroduction of Islam into the mass media is an interesting
    development. Esposito notes, 'ironically, the technological tools of
    modernisation have often served to reinforce traditional belief and
    practice as religious leaders who initially opposed modernisation
    now use radio, television and print to preach and disseminate, to
    educate and to proselytise. The message of Islam is not simply
    available from a preacher at a local mosque. Sermons and religious
    education from leading preachers and writers can be transmitted
    to every village' (Esposito 1983: 212).

17 In his essay on Muslim personalities in Malaysia and Indonesia,
    Stauth (2002) stresses the complexity of knowledge exchanges, the
    creativity of Muslim intellectuals, and the intercultural translation
    of 'Middle Eastern Islamic discourse'.

18 For a sound comparative perspective, see Stauth (2002) especially
    pp. 13-43.

Notes to Chapter 4

1   Her essays on Thai media will appear in a volume and will also contain her material on cults and rituals of the coastal Chinese in multicultural Southern Thailand. For a survey article see Hamilton (1992).

2   See Eickelman and Anderson (1999).

3   For a very detailed analysis of a Muslim newspaper in Indonesia, see Hefner (1997) on *Media Dakwah*.

4   For a more comprehensive discussion on mass media and Islam, see the papers that were presented at the conference, Mass Media and the Transformation of Islamic Discourse' (ISEAS, Leiden, 24 March 1997.)

5   For a focus on radio in Indonesia see Lindsay (1997).

6   Chang (1996: 57) writes that 'historical memory is not necessarily based upon the common experience of a particular historical event, it can also be recognised through the emotional participation in any ceremonial activities ... The focus is not on social interaction in conformity with an established historical memory but on individual choice. It refers to the dynamic feature of social solidarity.'

7   The pained historical consciousness is reflected throughout Ibrahim Syukri's (pseudonym) Sejarah Kerajaan Melayu Patani [History of the Malay Kingdom of Patani (1949)]. His historical anger is illuminating as a story of Pattani told by an educated and politically conscious Pattani Muslim. His position is described at the end of the book. He writes, 'If studied in depth, since the fall of Patani in the eighteenth century until this day, it is clear that the government of Siam has misgoverned during this whole period of time. No progress has been made in Patani to provide well-being for the Malays. In matters of health, education, association, and economy, Patani has lagged far behind the progress of its neighbours in Malaya. The actions of the Siamese government, which allow the Malays to live in backwardness, definitely gives a large profit to them, but this has grieved the hearts of the Malays' (Syukri 1985, pp. 75-76). The book was banned in Thailand and Malaysia, but was widely circulated in Patani at the time of my fieldwork.

8   The story of a curse is told by Ibrahim Syukri (1985: 31): 'With a broken heart she hanged herself from a cashew tree. Before taking her life, she issued a curse that the construction of *Kru Se* mosque would never be completed. The Chinese of Patani took her corpse and buried it according to the customs of their religion. They took the cashew tree and made an image of *Lim Gor Niew* which was then prayed to as a respected holy idol.'

9   'Communities of Practice' refer to the communal spaces in-between the domestic and the wider social institutions. 'Communities of Memory' refer to the same frame, in which the past can be re-enacted.

10 Dress is a coded sensory system of non-verbal communication; as such, dress includes visual as well as other sensory modifications (taste, smell, sound and touch) and supplements to the body which sets off cognitive and affective processes that result in recognition by the viewer (cf. Eicher 1995).

11 As Mulder (1998) shows, the Thai educational system teaches the place of people in society, teaches loyalty towards the nation and endorses a national imagined past. The educational system has a major role not only in disseminating the Thai language, but also an official version of the past. This is incribed into the Thai educational system.

12 The author of the book told me that he spent many months collecting materials in the archives of the old houses and the University. In addition, he carried out many interviews with older relatives. He also returned to China to collect material for a second volume.

13 The first international conference on Islamic Studies in ASEAN was held at Prince of Songkla University, Pattani Campus, July 1998.

14 Lewis (1975) notes that both festivals have at least some ostensible historical reference. The annual pilgrimage to Mekka evokes the memory of Muhammad. And Ramadan was selected because of its explicit historic references; it was in this month, the fifth of the Muslim year, that the Qur'an was sent down as a guide for the people. On appropriation of Muslim history see, Lewis (1975).

15 Connerton (1989: 58) writes: 'A curse seeks to bring its object under the sway of its power; once pronounced a curse continues to consign its object to the fate it has summoned up and is thought to continue in effect until its potency is exhausted'.

Notes to Chapter 5

1   Clues to a differentiation of a religious sphere are found in a sudden increase of new periodicals, whose titles and subtitles declare a specifically religious inspiration.

2   The transformation of Chinese spaces of representation and belonging are taken up again in the concluding remarks, relying partly

on fieldwork carried out by others (Hamilton 1999). However, the book focuses on Buddhist Muslim relationships.

3 Compare with Chapter 3: 'Alternative Organisation', in Callahan (1998).

4 Bourdieu (1979, 1991) argues that academics acquire a pedagogical authority in the field of education, allowing them to engage in symbolic forms of power.

Notes to Conclusion

1 I find myself in accordance with sociologists who study everyday life by means of qualitative methodologies (Amann/ Hirschauer 1997).

2 On the resurgence of moral discourse, see Eder's (2000) study on social movements.

3 One thinks here of Foucault's analysis of the body, discipline, sexuality, social control and bio-politics.

4 The leaders are very much aware of this incorporation; however, the organizations are dependent on the financial support of business corporations. Likewise, they want to overcome their isolation and participate in formal political institutions (Interview with Dr. Vichai Kanchanasuwon).

5 The mayor gave his address after a seminar of the sister organizations *Songkla Forum* and Bangkok Forum in May 1996.

6 I am grateful to Hamilton for pointing out the rise of the *Kwan Im* cult and the *Nine Emperor God* festivals in the south to me. Hamilton has done extensive research on the Chinese spirits and the accompanying media (Hamilton 1999).

7 On the interactions between the Middle East and Southeast Asia, see von der Mehden (1993) Riddell (2001) and Stauth (1999, 2002).

8 I am grateful to Suchira (1991: 249-250), who gives a detailed description of Bhudhadhasa's reinterpretation of Buddhism as well as a fine analysis of Buddhism as a way of life. The part on Bhuddhadasa's organization relies on her thesis.

9 The schedule of Phra Santikaro, the writings of Bhudhadhasa, and a user's list are available online: the address: www.suanmokkh.org (last visited on 22.02.2000). Cf. Chapter 4 on community media for details on the role of the accompanying media.

10 See Mannheim (1976), p. 36.

Bibliography

Abaza, Mona (1991a): "The discourse over Islamic fundamentalism in the Middle East and Southeast Asia. A critical perspective." SO-JOURN 6, No. 2, pp. 203-239.

Abdullah, Taufik/Siddique, Sharon (1986): *Islam and Society in Southeast Asia*. Singapore: Institute of Southeast Asian Studies.

Ackerman, Susan E./Lee, Raymond L. M. (eds.) (1988): *Heaven in Transition. Non-Muslim Religious Innovation and Ethnic Identity in Malaysia*. Honolulu: University of Hawaii Press.

Ahmed Akbar S./Donnan, Hastings (eds.) (1994): *Islam, Globalization and Postmodernity*. London and New York: Routledge.

Amann, Klaus/Hirschauer, Stefan (eds.) (1997): *Die Befremdung der eigenen Kultur. Zur ethnographischen Herausforderung soziologischer Empirie*. Frankfurt/Main: Suhrkamp.

Anderson, Benedict (1983): *Imagined Communities: Reflection on the Origin and Spread of Nationalism*. London: Verso.

Appadurai, Arjun (1995): "The Production of Locality". In: Richard Fardon (ed.): *Counterworks. Managing the Diversity of Knowledge*. London/New York: Routledge, pp. 204-225.

Arong Suthasasna (1976): *Problems of Conflict in the Four Southern Provinces*. Bangkok: Pitakpracha. (in Thai)

Bauman, Zygmunt (1995): *Life in Fragments. Essays in Postmodern Morality*. Oxford: Blackwell.

Bougas, Wayne A. (1994): *The Kingdom of Patani. Between Thai and Malay Mandalas*. Institute of the Malay World and Civilisation, Bangi: University Kebangsaan Malaysia.

Bourdieu, Pierre (1979): *La Distinction. Critique Sociale du Jugement*. Paris: Les Editions de Minuit.

Bourdieu, Pierre (1991): *Language and Symbolic Power.* Cambridge: Polity Press.

Bourdieu, Pierre/Wacquant, Loic J. D. (1992): *An Invitation to Reflexive Sociology.* Cambridge: Polity Press.

Bowie, Kathrin A. (1997): *Rituals of National Loyalty. An Anthropology of the State and the Village Scout Movement in Thailand.* New York: Columbia University Press.

Brown, David (1994): *The State and Ethnic Politics in South-East Asia.* London/New York: Routledge.

Calhoun, Craig (ed.) (1992): *Habermas and the Public Sphere.* Cambridge, MA: MIT Press.

Callahan, William A. (1998): *Imagining Democracy. Reading "the Events of May" in Thailand.* Singapore: Institute of Southeast Asian Studies.

Carsten, Janet (1998): "Borders, Boundaries, Tradition and State on the Malaysian Periphery." In: Thomas M. Wilson and Hastings Donnan (eds.): *Border Identities. Nation and State at International Frontiers.* Cambridge: Cambridge University Press, pp. 215-236.

Chai-Anan Samudavanija (1997): *Culture is Capital (Wattanatham kue tun).* Bangkok P. Press.

Chaiwat Satha-Anand (1992): "Pattani in the 1980s: Academic literature and political stories." SOJOURN 7, No 1, pp. 1-38.

Chaiwat Satha-Anand (1993): "Kru Se: A theatre for renegotiating Muslim identity." In: Hans-Dieter Evers: *Religious Revivalism in Southeast Asia.* In: SOJOURN 8, No. 1 (Special Issue), pp. 195-218.

Chaiwat Satha-Anand (1994): "Hijab and moments of legitimisation. Islamic resurgence in Thai society." In: Keyes, Charles F., Laurel Kendall, Helen Hardacre (eds.) (1994): *Asian Visions of Authority.* Honolulu: University of Hawaii Press, pp. 279-300.

Chang, Han-Pi (1997): *Taiwan, Community of Fate and Cultural Globalization.* Muenster: LIT (Market, Culture and Society 3).

Chatthip Nartsupah (1994): *Thai Culture and Social Change (Watthanatham Thai kap kabuan kanplianplaeng sangkhom).* Bangkok: Chulalongkorn University. (in Thai)

Chavivun Prachuabmoh (1980): *The Role of Women in maintaining ethnic identity and boundaries: a case of Thai-Muslims (the Malay Speaking Group) in Southern Thailand.* Unpublished Ph.D. Thesis, University of Hawaii Press.

Chavivun Prachuabmoh (ed.) (1993): *Four Decades of Southern Thailand: Social Transition, Culture and Political Development (1847-1993).* Bangkok: Thai Development Research Institute.

Chayan Rajchagool (1994): *The Rise and Fall of the Thai Absolute Monarchy.* Bangkok: White Lotus (Studies in Contemporary Thailand, Vol. 2).

Che Man, Wan Kadir (1983): *Muslim Elites and Politics in Southern Thailand.* Unpublished Masters Thesis, Penang: University Sains Malaysia.

Che Man, Wan Kadir (1990a): "The Thai government and Islamic institutions in the Four Southern Muslim provinces of Thailand." In: SOJOURN 5, No. 2, pp. 255-282.

Che Man, Wan Kadir (1990b): *Muslim Separatism: The Moros of Southern Phillipines and the Malays of Southern Thailand.* Singapore: Oxford University Press.

Chua, Beng Huat (ed.) (1999): *Consuming Asians: the Material Life of Asia's New Rich.* London/New York: Routledge.

Connerton, Paul (1989): *How societies remember.* Cambridge: Cambridge University Press.

Cushman, Jennifer W. (1991): *The Formation of a Sino-Thai Tin-Mining Dynasty 1797-1932.* Singapore: Oxford University Press.

Donnan, Hastings/Wilson, Thomas M. (eds.) (1998): "Nation, state and identity at international borders." In: ibid. (eds.): *Border Identities. Nation and State at International Frontiers.* Cambridge: Cambridge University Press.

Donnan, Hastings/Wilson, Thomas M. (1999): *Borders: Frontiers of Identity, Nation and State.* Oxford/New York: Berg.

Durrschmidt, Jorg (2001): *Everyday Lives in the Global City: The Delinking of Locale and Milieu.* London/New York: Routledge

Eicher, Joanne B. (1995): *Dress and Ethnicity: Change across Space and Time.* Oxford: Berg.

Eickelman, Dale F./Anderson, John W. (eds.) (1999): *New Media in the Muslim World. The Emerging Public Sphere.* Bloomington, Indiana: Indiana University Press.

Eickelman, Dale F./Piscatori, J. (eds.) (1990): *Muslim Travellers: Pilgrimage, Migration, and the Religious Imagination.* Berkeley: University of California Press.

Embong, Abdul Rahman (ed.) (2001): *Southeast Asian Middle Classes. Prospects for Social Change and Democratisation.* Bangi: Pernerbit University Kebangsaan Malaysia.

Esposito, John L. (1983): *Voices of Resurgent Islam.* Oxford: Oxford University Press.

Evans, Grant (1998): *The Politics of Ritual and Remembrance.* Laos since 1975. Chiang Mai: Silkworm Books.

Evers (1974): *Studies on Social Stratification in Southeast Asia.* WP No. 34, Department of Sociology. National University of Singapore.

Evers, Hans-Dieter/Schiel, Tilman (1988): *Strategische Gruppen. Vergleichende Studien zu Staat, Bürokratie und Klassenbildung in der Dritten Welt.* Berlin: Reimer.

Farouk, Omar Bajunid (1980): *The Political Integration of the Thai Islam.* Dissertation, University of Kent.

Farouk, Omar Bajunid (1994): *Muslim Social Sciences in ASEAN.* Kuala Lumpur: Yayasan Penataran Ilmu.

Fentress, Chris/Wickham, James (1992): *Social Memory.* Oxford: Blackwell (New perspectives on the past).

Foucault, Michel/Luther, Martin H. (eds.) (1988): *Technology of the Self: a Seminar with Michel Foucault.* London: Tavistock.

Fraser, Thomas (1966): *Fishermen of Southern Thailand. The Malay Villagers.* New York: Holt, Rinehart and Winston.

Friedman, Jonathan (1994): *Consumption and Identity.* Chur: Harwood Academic.

Frykman, Jonas/Löfgren, Orvar (1987): *Culture Builders: A Historical Anthropology of Middle-Class Life.* Rutgers University Press: New Brunswick and London.

Fukushima, Masato (1999): "Another meaning of meditation: On the Santi Asoke movement in Thailand." In: Horstmann, Alexander/Horstmann, Naomi (eds.): *Japanese Anthropologists and Tai*

Culture. Tai Culture. International Review on Tai Cultural Studies, Vol. IV, No. 1, pp. 131-152.

Gabaude, Louis (1979): *Introduction a l'Hermeneutique de Buddhadasa Bhikku*. Unpublished Ph.D. Thesis, La Sorbonne Nouvelle, Paris III.

Galizia, Michele (1996): "Die Entstehung und Entwicklung von Mittelklasse, Beamten und Ethnizität in Rejang-Lebong, südliches Sumatra." In: Internationales Asienforum, Vol. 27, No. 3-4: 241-267.

Geertz, Clifford (1968): *Islam Observed. Religious Development in Morocco and Indonesia*. The University of Chicago Press.

Gesick, Lorraine (1985): "Reading the landscape: Reflections on a sacred site in South Thailand." In: Journal of the Siam Society 73, No. 1-2 (January, July, 1985), pp. 157-61.

Gesick, Lorraine M. (1995): In the Land of Lady White Blood. *Southern Thailand and the Meaning of History*. Ithaca, New York: Cornell University Press (Southeast Asia Program).

Gledhill, John (1994): *Power and its Disguises: Anthropolical Perspectives on Politics*. London: Pluto Press.

Goffman, Erving (1959): *The Presentation of Self in Everyday Life*. Garden City, NY: Doubleday: Anchor Books.

Goffman, Erving (1974): *Frame Analysis: an Essay on the Organisation of Experience*. Cambridge: Harvard University Press.

Golomb, Louis (1978): *Brokers of Morality: Thai Ethnic Adaptation in a Rural Malaysian Setting*. Hawaii: The Univisity Press of Hawaii.

Habermas, Jürgen (1979): *Strukturwandel der Öffentlichkeit: Untersuchungen zu einer Kategorie der bürgerlichen Gesellschaft*. Neuwied: Luchterhand.

Halbwachs, Maurice (1950): *La Mémoire Collective. Ouvrage Posthume publie par Jeanne Alexandre née Halbwachs*. Paris: Presses Universitaires de France.

Halbwachs, Maurice (1952): *Les Cadres Sociaux de la Mémoire*. Paris: Presses Univ. de France.

Hamilton, Annette (1991): "Rumours, foul calumnies and the safety of the state: mass media and national Identity in Thailand." In:

Reynolds, Craig J. (1991): *National Identity and its Defenders. Thailand, 1939-1989*. Chiangmai: Silkworm Books, pp. 341-378.

Hamilton, Annette (1992): "The Mediascape of Modern Southeast Asia." In: Screen 33: No 1, pp. 81-92.

Hamilton, Annette (1999): "Kwan Im, Nine Emperor Gods, and Chinese Spirit in Southern Thailand." Paper presented to the 7th International Conference on Thai Studies, Amsterdam, 4-8 July 1999.

Hann, Chris (ed.) (1996): *Civil Society: Challenging Western Models*. London and New York: Routledge.

Hannerz, Ulf (1992): *Cultural Complexity. Studies in the Social Organisation of Meaning*. New York: Columbia University Press.

Hannerz, Ulf (1996): *Transnational Connections*. Routledge: London and New York.

Hefner, Robert W. (1997): "Print Islam: Mass Media and Ideological Rivalries among Indonesian Muslims." In: Indonesia, No 64, October 1997, pp. 77-103.

Herzfeld, Michael (1997): *Cultural Intimacy. Social Poetics in the Nation-State*. London/New York: Routledge.

Hobsbawm, Eric (1983): "Introduction: inventing traditions." In: Eric Hobsbawm and Terence Ranger (eds.): *The Invention of Tradition*. Cambridge: Cambridge University Press, pp. 1-14.

Horstmann, Alexander (1999a): "Communities of practice, communities of interest: The making of consumers in Southern Thailand." In: Richard Fardon, Wim van Binsbergen and Rijk van Dijk: *Modernity on a Shoestring. Dimensions of globalization, consumption and development in Africa and beyond*. Leiden & London: EIDOS, pp. 281-299.

Horstmann, Alexander (1999b): "Mittelschichten und Zivilgesellschaft in Suedthailand." In: Bert Becker, Juergen Rueland, Nikolaus Werz (Hrsg.): *Mythos Mittelschichten. Zur Wiederkehr eines Paradigmas der Demokratieforschung*. Bonn: Bouvier, pp. 228-241.

Horstmann, Alexander (1999c): "Visions, claims and utopias: re-negotiating social space for Muslims in Patani." In: Stauth, Georg/Buchholt, Helmut (eds.): *Investigating the South-South Dimension of Modernity and Islam: Circulating Visions and Ideas, Intellectual Figures,*

Locations. Yearbook of the Sociology of Islam, 2. Hamburg: LIT, pp. 191-211.

Horstmann, Alexander (1999d): "Reconceptualizing civil society. performing public culture." In: Proceedings, 7th International Conference on Thai Studies, 04-08 July 1999, Amsterdam.

Horstmann, Alexander (2000): *The Making of a New Middle Class: Social Space and the Construction and Consumption of Cultural Images in Southern Thailand.* Ph.D. Thesis, Faculty of Sociology, University of Bielefeld.

Horstmann, Alexander/Schlee, Guenther (eds.) (2001a): *Integration durch Verschiedenheit: Lokale und globale Formen inter-kultureller Kommunikation.* Transkript: Bielefeld.

Horstmann, Alexander (2001b): "Wertschaetzung und Aechtung: Moral and Politik in Suedthailand." In: Internationales Asienforum 32, No. 3-4, pp. 337-360.

Horstmann, Alexander (2002a): "Rethinking citizenship: identities at the fringe of the nation-state in national and post-national times." In: Proceedings, 8th International Conference on Thai Studies, Nakhorn Phanom,

Horstmann, Alexander (forthcoming): "Incorporation and resistence: borderlands and social transformation in Southeast Asia (Review article)." In: Anthropologi Indonesia. Indonesian Journal of Social and Cultural Anthropology, Padang 26, No. 67, January-April 2002.

Hurgronje, Christian Snouk (1931): *Mecca in the Latter Part of the 19th Century.* London.

Jackson, Peter A. (1989): *Buddhism, Legitimation, and Conflict. The Political Functions of Urban Thai Buddhism.* Singapore: Institute of Southeast Asian Studies.

Kahn, Joel S. (1991): "Constructing culture: towards an anthropology of the middle classes in Southeast Asia." In: Asian Studies Review 15, No. 2, pp. 50-56.

Kahn, Joel S. (1992): "Class, ethnicity and diversity: some remarks on Malay culture in Malaysia." In: Joel S. Kahn and Francis Loh Kok Wah (eds.): *Fragmented Vision. Culture and Politics in Contemporary Malaysia.* Honolulu: Hawaii University Press.

Kahn, Joel S. (1995): "The middle class as a field of ethnological study." In: Ikmal Said and Zahin Emby (eds.): *Critical Perspectives: Essays in Honour of Syed Hussin Ali*. Kuala Lumpur: Malaysian Social Science Association.

Kahn, Joel S. (1998): *Southeast Asian Identities: Culture and the Politics of Representation in Indonesia, Malaysia, Singapore and Thailand*. Singapore: Institute for Southeast Asian Studies (ISEAS).

Kanchana Kaewthep: Media: *The Mirror of Culture* (*Sue song Watthanatham*). Bangkok: Amarin Publishing. (in Thai)

Karim, Wazir Jahan (1992): *Women and Culture: Between Malay Adat and Islam*. Boulder: Westview Press.

Kessler, Clive S. (1978): *Islam and Politics in a Malay State. Kelantan 1838-1969*. Ithaca and London: Cornell University Press.

Keyes, Charles (1987): *Thailand: Buddhist Kingdom as Modern Nation-State*. Boulder, Colorado: Westview Press.

Kobkua Suwannathat-Pian (1988): *Thai-Malay Relations. Traditional Intra-regional Relations from the Seventeenth to the Early Twentieth Centuries*. Singapore: Oxford University Press.

Kraus, Werner (1984): *Islam in Thailand: Notes on the History of Muslim Provinces, Thai Islamic Modernism and the Separatist Movement in the South*. In: Journal- Institute of Muslim Minority Affairs 5, 2, pp. 410-25.

Lamont, Michele (1992): *Money, Morals and Manners: the Culture of the French and American Upper-Middle Class*. Chicago: University of Chicago Press.

Le Roux, Pierre (1994): *L'Elephant Blanc aux Defenses Noires. Mythes et Identite Chez les Jawi, Malais de Patani (Thailande du Sud)*, Tome 1-2. Unpublished Ph.D. Thesis, Paris: Ecole des Hautes Etudes en Sciences Sociales.

Lee, Raymond L. M./Ackerman, Susan (eds.) (1997): *Sacred Tensions. Modernity and Religious Transformation in Malaysia*. Columbia, South Carolina: University of South Carolina Press.

Lefebvre, Henri (1974): *La Production de l'Espace*. Paris: Ed. Anthropos.

Lewis, Bernard (1975): *History: Remembered, Recorded, Invented*. Princeton: Princeton University Press.

Lindsay, Jennifer (1997): "Making waves: private radio and local identities in Indonesia." In: Indonesia, No 64, October 1997, pp. 105-123

Lovell, Nadia ed. (1998): *Locality and Belonging*. London and New York: Routledge.

Maaruf, Shaharuddin (1999): "Religion and utopian thinking among the Muslims of Southeast Asia." Paper presented to the 4th Inter-University ASEAN Seminar on Social Development, Pattani, 14-16.06.1999.

Madmarn, Hasan (1990): *Traditional Muslim Institutions in Southern Thailand: A Critical Study of Islamic Education and Arabic Influence in the Pondok and Madrasah Systems of Pattani*, Ph.D. Thesis, University of Utah.

Madmarn, Hasan (1999): *The Pondok and Madrasah in Patani*. Bangi: Penerbit University Kebangsaan Malaysia.

Madmarn, Saynee (1988): *Language Use and Loyalty among the Malays Muslims of Southern Thailand*. Unpublished Ph.D. Thesis, State University of New York at Buffalo.

Matheson, V./Hooker, M. B. (1988): "Jawi literature in Patani: the maintenance of an Islamic tradition." In: Journal of the Malaysian Branch of the Royal Asiatic Society 61 (254), pp. 1-86.

Morley, David/Robins, Kevin (1997): *Spaces of Identity: Global Media, Electronic Landscapes and Cultural Boundaries*. London and New York: Routledge.

Mulder, Niels (1993): "The urban educated middle stratum and religion in Southeast Asia." In: Hans-Dieter Evers and Sharon Siddique (eds.): *Religious Revivalism in Southeast Asia*. SOJOURN 8, No. 1, February, Special Focus, pp. 184-194.

Mulder, Niels (1997): *Thai Images. The Culture of the Public World*. Chiang Mai: Silkworm Books.

Müller, Hans-Peter (1993): *Sozialstruktur und Lebensstile. Der neuere theoretische Diskurs über soziale Ungleichheit*. Frankfurt: Suhrkamp.

Mutalib, Hussin (1990): *Islam and Ethnicity in Malay Politics*. Singapore: Oxford University Press.

Nagata, Judith (1974): "What is a Malay? Situational selection of ethnic identity in a plural society." In: American Ethnologist No. 1, pp. 331-50.

Nagata, Judith (1984): *The Reflowering of Malaysian Islam. Modern Religious Radicals and their Roots.* Vancouver: University of British Columbia Press.

Nagata, Judith (1994): "How to be Islamic without being an Islamic State: Contested models of development, law and morality in Malaysia." In: Akbar, Ahmad and Hastings Donnan (eds.): *Islam, Postmodernism and Globalization*, London and New York: Routledge, pp. 63-90.

Nishii, Ryoko (1999): "Coexistence of religions: Muslim and Buddhist relationship on the West Coast of Southern Thailand." In: Alexander Horstmann/Naomi Horstmann (eds.) (1999): *Japanese Anthropologists and Tai Culture.* Tai Culture. International Review on Tai Cultural Studies. (4) 1, June 1999, pp. 77-92.

Nishii, Ryoko (2001): *Death and Practical Religion. Perspectives on Muslim-Buddhist Relationship in Southern Thailand.* Tokyo: Research Institute of Languages and Cultures of Asia and Africa (ILCAA). (in Japanese)

Nishii, Ryoko (2002a): "Social memory as it emerges. A consideration of the death of a young convert on the West coast in Southern Thailand." In: Tanabe, Shigeharu/Keyes, Charles (2002): Cultural Crisis and Social Memory: Politics of the Past in the Thai World. Richmond: Curzon Press, pp. 231-242.

Nishii, Ryoko (2002b): "A way of negotiating with the other within the self: Muslim acknowledgement of Buddhist ancestors in Southern Thailand." Paper presented to the First Inter-Dialogue Conference on Southern Thailand: Experiencing Southern Thailand. Current Transformations from a People's Perspective, 13-15 June 2002, Prince of Songkla University, Pattani Campus and Department of Social Anthropology, Harvard University.

Nora, Pierre (1984): *Les Lieux de Mémoire.* Paris: Gallimard.

Ockey, Jim (1992): *Business Leaders, Gangsters, and the Middle Class: Societal Groups and Civilian Rule in Thailand.* Unpublished Ph.D. Thesis, Cornell University.

Ockey, Jim (1999): "Creating the Thai middle class." In: Pinches, Michael (ed.) (1999): *Culture and Privilege in Capitalist Asia.* London and New York: Routledge (New Rich in Asia), pp. 230-250.

Ong, Aihwa (1995): *Bewitching Women, Pious Men. Gender and Body Politics in Southeast Asia.* Berkeley: University of California Press.

Panpimon Sarochamad (1995): *The Role of Muslim Newspaper in Thailand (Botbat nangsuepim Muslim nai prathes Thai).* Unpublished Master Thesis, Department of Journalism and Mass Communication, Chulalongkorn University. (in Thai)

Pasuk Phongpaichit/Baker, Chris (1995): *Thailand. Economy and Politics.* Kuala Lumpur: Oxford University Press.

Pertierra, Raul (ed.) (1999): *Asian Values.* SOJOURN 14, No. 2.

Phuwadol Songprasert (1993): "The investment of Malaysian-Chinese in southern Thailand." In: *Thailand and her Neighbors*, 19-20 November 1993, Siran Kaikan, Sakyo, Kyoto.

Piriyarangsan, Sungsidh and Pasuk Phongpaichit eds. (1993): *The Middle Class and Thai Democracy (chon chan klang kap prachathipatai Thai).* Political Economy Centre and Friedrich-Ebert-Foundation: Chulalongkorn University. (in Thai)

Prawes Wasi (1999): *The Self-Sufficient Economy and Civil Society: The way to Restore the Economy and Society.* Bangkok: Mor Chaoban. (in Thai)

Preyer, Gerhard/Boes, Matthias (eds.) (2001): *On a Sociology of Borderlines: Social Process in Time of Globalization.* In: Proto Sociology. An International Journal of Interdisciplinary Research, Vol. 15 (2001).

Prodolliet, Simone (1996): "Die Mittelklasse in der indonesischen Provinz: Eine Fallstudie über Ökonomie und Lebensstil der Mittelklasse in einer Kleinstadt im Südwesten Sumatras." Internationales Asienforum 27, No. 3-4: pp. 269-299.

Purushotam, Nirmala (1998): "Between compliance and resistance: women and the middle-class way of life in Singapore." In: Stivens, Maila/Sen, Krishna: *Gender and Power in Affluent Asia.* London/New York: Routledge, pp. 127-166.

Rajah, Ananda and Amitav Acharya (eds.) (1999): *Reconceptualising Southeast Asia.* Southeast Asian Journal of Social Science, Vol. 27, No. 1 (Special Focus).

Reynolds, Craig J. (ed.) (1991): *National Identity and its Defenders. Thailand, 1939-1989.* Chiang Mai: Silkworm Books.

Riddell, Peter G. (2001): *Islam and the Malay-Indonesian World. Transmission and Responses*. London: Hurst

Robison, Richard and David Goodman (eds.) (1996): *The New Rich in Asia: Mobile Phones, McDonalds and Middle-Class Revolution*. London/ New York: Routledge.

Roff, William R. (1967): *The Origins of Malay Nationalism*. New Haven: Yale University Press

Roff, William R. (ed.) (1974): *Kelantan. Religion, Society and Politics in a Malay State*. Kuala Lumpur: Oxford University Press.

Rudie, Ingrid (1994): *Visible Women in East Coast Malay Society. On the Reproduction of Gender in Ceremonial, School and Market*. Oslo: Scandinavian University Press.

Rüland Jürgen (1999): "Janusköpfige Mittelschichten in Südostasien." In: Becker, Bert/Rüland, Juergen/Werz, Nikolaus (eds.): *Mythos Mittelschichten. Zur Wiederkehr eines Paradigmas der Demokratieforschung*. Bonn: Bouvier, pp. 41 75.

Said, Edward W. (1994): *Orientalism*. New York: Pantheon Books.

Salvatore, Armando (1997): *Islam and the Political Discourse of Modernity*. Reading: Ithaca Press.

Salvatore, Armando (1998): "Staging virtue: the disembodiment of self-correctness and the making of Islam as public norm." In: Stauth, Georg (ed.): *Islam- Motor or Challenge of Modernity*. Hamburg: Lit: 87-120.

Schlee, Günther/Karin Werner (1996): *Inklusion und Exklusion: Die Dynamik von Grenzziehungen im Spannungsfeld von Markt, Staat und Ethnizität*. Köln: Rüdiger Köppe Verlag.

Schütz, Alfred/Thomas Luckmann (1979): *Strukturen der Lebenswelt*. Bd. 1 und Bd. 2. Frankfurt/Main: Suhrkamp.

Scupin, Raymond (1998): "Muslim accomodation in Thai society." In: Journal of Islamic Studies 9, No. 2, pp. 229-258.

Sen, Krishna/Stivens, Maila (eds.) (1998): *Gender and Power in Affluent Asia*. London/New York: Routledge.

Sirirat Thanirananont/Donmanat Baka/Chalongpob Susangkornkan (eds.) (1995): *The Participation of Thai Muslims in Social and Economic Development. A Case Study of Lower Southern Thailand*. Bangkok: Thai Development Research Institute.

Sivaraksa, Sulak (1988): *A Socially Engaged Buddhism*. Bangkok: Inter-Religious Commission for Development.

Stauth, Georg/Turner, Bryan S. (1988a): *Nietzsche's Dance. Resentment, Reciprocity and Resistance in Social Life*. Oxford: New York: Basil Blackwell.

Stauth, Georg/Turner, Bryan S. (1988b): "Nostalgia, postmodernism and the critique of mass culture." In: Theory, Culture and Society 5, No. 2/3, pp. 509-526.

Stauth, Georg (1999): *Authentizität und Kulturelle Globalisierung*. Bielefeld: Transcript Publishers.

Stauth, Georg/Buchholt, Helmut (eds.) (1999): *Investigating the South-South Dimension of Modernity and Islam: Circulating Visions and Ideas, Intellectual Figures, Locations*. In: Yearbook of the Sociology of Islam, 2.

Stauth, Georg (2002): *Politics and Cultures of Islamization in Southeast Asia. Indonesia and Malaysia in the Nineteen-nineties*. Bielefeld. Transcript Publishers.

Stivens, Maila (1996): *Matriliny and Modernity: Sexual Politics and Social Change in Rural Malaysia*. Asian Studies Association of Australia. Women in Asia Series. Sydney: Allen & Unwin.

Stivens, Maila (1998a): "Theorising gender, power and modernity in affluent Asia." In: Sen, Krishna/Stivens, Maila: *Gender and Power in Affluent Asia*. London and New York: Routledge, pp. 1-34.

Stivens, Maila (1998b): "Sex, gender and the making of the new Malay middle classes." In: Krishna Sen/Stivens, Maila: *Gender and Power in Affluent Asia*. London and New York: Routledge, pp. 87-126.

Suchart Sriyaranya (1999b): *Thai intellectuals: Critical role and alternative discourse in the public life of Thailand*. Unpublished Ph.D. Thesis. Faculty of Sociology, University of Bielefeld.

Suchira Payulpitack (1991): *Bhudhadhasa's Movement: An Analysis of its Origins, Development, and Social Impact*. Unpublished Ph.D. Thesis, Faculty of Sociology, University of Bielefeld.

Surin Maisrikrod (1999): "Joining the value debate. the peculiar case of Thailand." In: Pertiarra, Raul (ed.): Asian Values. SOJOURN 14, No. 2, pp. 402-13.

Surin Pitsuwan (1985): *Islam and Malay Nationalism: A Case Study of the Malay Muslims of Southern Thailand*. Bangkok: Thai Khadi Research Institute, Thammasat University (in Thai).

Swearer, Donald K. (1995): *The Buddhist World of Southeast Asia*. Albany: State University of New York Press.

Syukri, Ibrahim (Pseudonym) (1985): *History of the Malay Kingdom of Patani*. Transl. by Baily, Connor/Miksic, John N.. Athens, Ohio: Ohio University Centre for International Studies.

Tambiah, Stanley Jeyaraja (1976): *World Conqueror and World Renouncer. A Study of Buddhism and Polity in Thailand Against a Historical Background*. Cambridge, Mass.: Cambridge University Press.

Tanter, Richard/ Young, Kenneth (eds.) (1990): *The Politics of Middle Class Indonesia*. Clayton: Monash Papers of Southeast Asia, No. 19.

Taylor, J. L. (1990): "New Buddhist movements in Thailand: An individualistic Revolution. Reform and Political Dissonance". In: Journal of Southeast Asian Studies 21 (1), pp. 135-54.

Taylor, J. L. (1993): *Forest Monks and the Nation-State. An Anthropological and Historical Study in Northeastern Thailand*. Singapore: Institute of Southeast Asian Studies.

Teeuw A./Wyatt, David K. (eds.) (1970): *Hykayat Patani. The Story of Patani*. The Hague. Martinus Nijhoff.

Thongchai Winichakul (1994): *Siam Mapped. A History of the Geo-Body of a Nation*. Chiang Mai: Silkworm Books.

Thrift, Nigel (1996): *Spatial Formations*. London: Sage.

Ubonrath Siriyuvasak (1999): "The media, cultural politics and the nation-state." Paper presented to the 7th International Conference on Thai Studies, Amsterdam, 4-8 July 1999.

Uthai Dulyakasem (1986): "The emergence and escalation of ethnic nationalism: the case of the Muslim Malays in Southern Siam." In: Abdullah, Taufik and Sharon Siddique (eds.): *Islam and Society in Southeast Asia*. Singapore: Institute of Southeast Asian Studies.

Vandergeest, Peter (1990): *Siam into Thailand. Constituting Progress, Resistance, and Citizenship*. Ph. D. Diss., Cornell University.

Vandergeest, Peter (1993): "Constructing Thailand: regulation, everyday resistance, and citizenship." Comparative Studies in Society and History 35 (1): pp. 133-58.

Vichai Kanchanasuwon (1998): *People's Organisations in the Development Process of Southern Thailand*. Report to the National Council of Social and Economic Development. Hatyai: Prince of Songkla University.

Vichai Kanchanasuwon (1999): *Project for Political Reform in Songkla, Thailand*. Songkla: Songkla: Provincial network for political reform (ungkorn prachathipatai nai changwat Songkla).

von der Mehden, Fred (1993): *The Two Worlds of Islam. Interaction between Southeast Asia and the Middle East*. Gainsville: University Press of Florida.

Welch, David J./Mc Neil, Judith R. (1989): "Archeological investigations of Pattani history." In: Journal of Southeast Asian Studies 20, 1: 27-41.

Worawit Baru (Ahmad Idris) (1995): *Tradition and Cultural Background of the Patani Region*. In: Volker Grabowski (ed.): Regional and National Integration in Thailand 1892-1992.

Zaleha, Sharifah Syed Hassan/Cederoth, Sven (1996): *Managing Marital Disputes in Malaysia: Islamic Mediators and Conflict Resolution in Syariah Courts*. Richmond: Curzon Press.

Horstmann, Alexander
Class, Culture and Space
The Construction and Shaping of Communal Space in South Thailand

15.08.2002
Research Institute for the Languages and Cultures of Asia and Africa (ILCAA)
(Southeast Asian Regional/Cultural Studies)
Tokyo University of Foreign Studies
(Tokyo Gaikokugo Daigaku)
3-11-1 Asahi-cho, Fuchu-shi, Tokyo 183-8534, Japan.

Bielefeld, Univ., Diss., 2000
ISBN: 4-87297-818-8

Typesetting: Camera-ready by the author
Printing and binding: Nikkei Printing, Japan
Production: Springer-Verlag, Tokyo, Japan
© Dr. Alexander Horstmann, 2002
ISBN: 4-87297-818-8